# The Last Rocketman

# THE LAST ROCKETMAN

A Memoir

DAN SCHLUND

BROWN BOOKS
PUBLISHING GROUP

*The Last Rocketman: A Memoir*

Brown Books Publishing Group
Dallas, TX / New York, NY
www.BrownBooks.com
(972) 381-0009

A New Era in Publishing®

Publisher's Cataloging-In-Publication Data

Names: Schlund, Dan, author.
Title: The last rocketman : a memoir / Dan Schlund.
Description: Dallas, TX ; New York, NY : Brown Books Publishing Group, [2025] | Includes index.
Identifiers: LCCN: 2025939001 | ISBN: 9781612547473 (hardcover) | 9781612547497 (ePub)
Subjects: LCSH: Schlund, Dan. | Air pilots--United States--Biography. | Stunt performers--United States--Biography. | Allied health personnel--United States--Biography. | Personal propulsion units--Piloting. | LCGFT: Autobiographies. | BISAC: BIOGRAPHY & AUTOBIOGRAPHY / Adventurers & Explorers. | SELF-HELP / Personal Growth / Happiness. | BIOGRAPHY & AUTOBIOGRAPHY / Religious.
Classification: LCC: TL540.S336 A3 2025 | DDC: 629.13092--dc23

ISBN 978-1-61254-747-3
EISBN 978-1-61254-749-7
LCCN 2025939001

Printed in Canada
10 9 8 7 6 5 4 3 2 1

For more information or to contact the author, please go to www.TheLastRocketman.com.

To all the dreamers big, small, young, and old. The adventures and non-adventurers alike. We all have dreams and not pursuing those dreams leads to regrets. Live life to the fullest. You will get hurt, you will lose, and you will win; nothing is guaranteed.

To Kinnie and Sheri Gibson for offering me the opportunity to live this dream and giving me words of encouragement when I was least confident.

To God, who is the one guide who won't leave your side when things go bad. There are many blessings stored up for you if you just dare to have faith and pray.

Finally, to my son Danny, and his children, grandchildren, and so on down the line.

Let this book be an inspiration and cautionary tale to all who read it.

I know people say it but it's true: You can do anything you set your mind to, and sometimes you can't do it alone—but that doesn't mean that it's not possible.

—Danny Schlund, age 12, from the documentary *The Last Rocketman*

# Table of Contents

# Author's Note

When you see the Rocketman take to the sky, you are witness to a graceful, peaceful flight. A human experiencing the joy of freedom without a care in the world, flying to and from, wherever and whenever he wants. Soaring and spinning like a bird—literally playing in the air.

The Rocketman persona is built from a dream of flight, a thirst for adventure, and an extraordinary wellspring of courage in the face of physical danger. But there's far more involved than that. Few are willing to do what it takes to experience this feat, even with these qualities, once they realize the sacrifices and risks involved—the practice, the procedures, the planning, and the ever-present possibility of crashing or even death, which are part of the job every day. After all, every Rocketbelt pilot has crashed at some point.

In a way, I am the last Rocketman. While there is a new generation of jet-pack pilots out there—men and women who have taken the solo jet-propulsion dream to new heights and new technologies I could have never imagined—I am the last of a small clique of risk-takers to have learned the art of carrying out a Rocketman performance to a global audience when none other existed. I am the last of a short line of trailblazers who dared strap what was nothing shy of an actual rocket motor on their back just for the thrill of possibly achieving flight for less than thirty seconds. And I am the last of the cowboys from a subculture of a subculture to have been called a "Rocketbelt pilot" despite having no formal education or any kind of degree to warrant such a title. And for this, I am proud.

# Acknowledgments

I am incredibly grateful to those who encouraged, inspired and even pushed me along my journey. Most notably, I'd like to thank my parents. It was my mom who encouraged me to see the world. She was by my side during those long hospital stays, and it was my dad who covered my bills during the most difficult times.

It was with Dave Kilde, my partner in "stunt" crime, that I honed my stunt skills and provided opportunities I would have never had on my own.

My former wife Shelley also deserves my most effusive gratitude. Not only did she believe in me before anyone else, it was my desire for her affection at a young age that drove me to be bigger and better than I was. She gave me a shoulder to cry on and words of encouragement.

I'd also like to thank the late Kinnie Gibson for choosing me and training me. You were much more than a boss and partner. You were a kindred spirit. And of course, Kinnie's widow, Sheri Gibson, who was the first person to see potential in me so many years ago and introduce me to Kinnie, even standing up for me in times of contention.

I would also like to thank Kinnie's brother, Shannon Gibson, who was my flight director and confidant, as well as all the members of the Rocketman team who did everything they could to keep me safe and grounded.

A special thank-you to Eric Scott, who not only accepted me onto the team but, as a fellow Rocketman, lent an ear and calming voice to all my concerns as only one Rocketman to another can. Being the best Rocketbelt pilot in history, he also helped coach me back into the air for the documentary, stating: "Dan's just got some cobwebs in his head he needs to shake out."

A few names especially come to mind when it comes to Rocketbelt technicians I've worked with through the years, those who kept me safe, those who encouraged me to go bigger, those whose focus and skill my life depended on: Sid Goodloe, Jeff Ayo, Bill Reed, stuntman Dave Kilde, and my late friend and co-stunt performer, Brian Nelson.

Additionally, this book would not be possible without the collaboration of my friend P.G. Cuschieri. Paul not only helped me write this book but also contributed to the documentary it inspired, *The Last Rocketman*. To that point, I would also like to thank Eric Dunn, executive producer; Jonny Zeller, director; Tatiana Kelly, producer; and associate producers Kevin Baldwin and Angelo Keys, for their dedication, friendship and hard work during the production of the documentary. This book and documentary would not be the success it is without their efforts, leadership, and friendship.

Thank you to Alan Burnce for helping me polish this book and work out all the rough edges.

Additionally, thank you to Milli Brown of Brown Books Publishing Group for believing in me, choosing to take me on, and mandating the fast-pacing of this book's production. Thanks as well to her team, including Brittany Griffiths and Amy Goppert, in guiding me on my book journey. A special thank-you to Ben Davidoff for his copyediting skills that helped bring the final edit to print. Because of them the story of *The Last Rocketman* will live on in print as well as on screen.

Finally, I'd like to thank my son, Danny, for which this book is written. Danny, you've given me flight in ways that I never knew existed. Being your father is my greatest achievement—my most important persona. You are and forever will be my greatest accomplishment and love of my life. (On a side note, both PaPa and your dad have scars on their right thighs; it's a tradition you don't have to continue.)

As a final prologue to my story that follows, I have to give thanks and praise to my Lord and Savior, Jesus Christ. A lot of people may think that I had just found God after having lived the wild and spectacular life of a Rocketman. Or that I finally crawled to him after so many close and horrific brushes with death. But the fact is, He has been with me from before the very beginning of my journey to my becoming Rocketman. He was there during the glorious times. He waited by my side as I made mistakes. And he stayed with me as I pieced myself together after each fall—lifting me up and protecting me. He is the reason that I am not defined by being a Rocketman but rather defined by Him. During all my life, I never strayed from believing in you or thought, "Why me?"

—Dan Schlund aka "The Rocketman," May 2025

# Preface

On April 20, 1961, Hal Graham performed the first ever free flight of the Rocketbelt. And almost forty-two years to that same date I performed my first tether-free flight of the Rocketbelt, making me only the eleventh person ever to be called a "Rocketman." To put this in perspective: More people have walked on the moon than have professionally flown a Rocketbelt.

When done right, an audience sees a Rocketbelt pilot fly with seemingly impossible grace. It looks fun and carefree, like a bird gliding on a thermal. In truth, it's a calculated and choregraphed dance in the sky requiring intense concentration, a steady hand, and an appetite for the potential for disaster that lurks at every stage. The illusion is something many want to experience but few are willing to take the risk for, and still fewer ever get the opportunity.

As a teenager and young man, I never drank or did illegal drugs. I never even smoked marijuana. My drug of choice was adrenaline, and I was an addict, a risk-taker. But the series of risks I took as far back as my childhood led me to an opportunity that only a handful of people in over fifty years have ever gotten. Little did I know that setting myself on fire, jumping off high platforms a thousand times, riding motorcycles, scuba diving, skydiving, and producing stunt shows in foreign countries were all preparing me for a truly unique career.

I wouldn't call myself a daredevil. I was just working on being a highly trained stunt professional. I absolutely loved the challenge of doing something many were afraid to do, to push the limits of my body and mind. It was that adrenaline rush that kept me pushing forward. And though I'd made many stupid decisions on my journey to piloting the Rocketbelt, I'd never hurt myself. I had found that fine line between pushing the envelope and surviving, and I loved riding it. I had convinced myself that I could achieve anything I set my mind to; if I worked hard, practiced, and took precautions I would gain mastery over it.

But the Rocketbelt was an entirely different beast where all my combined skills, including new ones I'd have to learn, would be needed to fly it. I paid for that journey with pain, scars, burn tissue, broken bones, and crippling anxiety. Being a Rocketman taught me that I was not as invincible as I'd once thought. But I was determined, well-trained, and persistent. The crashes I'd experience were just part of the job, and to give up after all the abuse my body and mind took was not an option. Would I do it all over again knowing what I know now? Yes, in a heartbeat.

## PART ONE

# VERTICAL DREAMS

And surely I am with you always, to the very end of the age.
—Matthew 28:20

# 1

# God Had Other Plans

I am neither the biggest dreamer nor the greatest risk-taker that my family has ever produced. The truth is, those traits were destined to be part of my personality long before I was born. But those traits are only the by-products of something much larger within me. There is another component to what has made me who I am that was as etched into the double helix of my DNA as my eye color.

Struggle.

I'm sure it goes back even further, but it was my great grandfather who was known as my family's first great risk-taker. He came to this country not even knowing how to speak its language—just to make a better life for him and his family. His children lived through the Great Depression and a world at war. And my own father had to fight in one too, in Vietnam. The matriarchs of our family didn't have it any easier either. They had to cook, clean, and raise their children. People often look back nostalgically and think of times past as easier, carefree, innocent. But nothing could be further from the truth. People faced incredible challenges. I honestly believe that had my family not faced the struggles they had, I would have never survived the struggles I myself have faced. And as I've lived long enough to reflect on it all, I am immeasurably grateful for those struggles. Not only did they stimulate my resolve and help fuel my determination, they actually brought me closer to God and, ultimately, made the triumphs all the more joyful.

My father was the first person in my life who for me embodied triumph over struggle. Throughout my childhood I only knew him as a dad who worked as an LAPD motorcycle officer. Yes, he was a devout Catholic who always carried a rosary in his pocket and was never short on prayer cards, too. He taught me how to pray, about guardian angels, and he told me the stories of the Bible. Early on, I believed in Jesus and felt His presence. The first prayer I remember saying when I was young was that I wanted to share all my good and adventurous experiences with Him. Little did I know at the time that His adventurous spirit ran deeper and faster than I could imagine.

But there was something else inside of my father, too. Something I could feel, but couldn't see. As children, we actually know very little about our parents. We just know that they're present all the time and boss us around while taking care of us. We hear things and see hints at another life beyond that of what we know, but we're generally too self-absorbed or just not curious enough to really find out more about them. Such was the case with my father. I knew there was something in his life beyond the vocation of being a dad to me and my two brothers, beyond being a husband to my mother, but I never knew what it was.

Finally, one day I figured it out. I must've been eight or nine. I had known Dad had been in the Army, and I'd seen a bunch of pictures of him in his uniform and his medals, but I never really knew his story. I then discovered that much of his story happened before I was even born.

I suppose Dad's life began to take shape in 1959, when he was fresh out of high school and figuring out what he wanted to do with his life. He joined the California Army National Guard and enrolled in the Los Angeles Police Academy. While serving his country and studying to be a lawman, he also decided that he'd like to get married. And, as fate would have it, there was a beautiful woman who drew his attention—and who just happened to live in his apartment complex—in fact, right next door. After months of building up the courage to ask her out, one day he finally marched over to her place and knocked with the intention of taking her to dinner.

But God had other plans.

The gal my dad was looking for wasn't home at the time, so her roommate answered the door instead. Her name was Sharon, and she was a flight attendant, which explained why my father hadn't seen her around much. He took her out instead.

Within the next year, my father was married, began working for the LAPD in its North Hollywood division, and my mom was pregnant. Dad's life had suddenly taken off—

But just as quick, things took a drastic turn. My father's National Guard unit was activated to go to Vietnam. At that time, a lot of young men were being drafted. And a lot of young men weren't coming back—58,220 in total by the end of the war. My mother and grandmother were petrified that he would be one of them. Because on top of being activated as an infantry sergeant in the Army, Dad was also sent to a particularly dangerous location in the Mekong Delta, south of Saigon.

As a point of fact, one out of every ten American soldiers who served in Vietnam was killed. On top of that, just over 14 percent of servicemen were wounded or severely disabled. And given that my father was deployed in a particularly dangerous area against a determined enemy force, I imagine those numbers might have been even higher. But even if they weren't, I had a pretty good chance of either growing up without a father or growing up with a father who may have suffered from any number of physical or emotional traumas. Not to mention that my two younger brothers wouldn't have even been born had he died there.

But God had other plans.

On one particular mission when a Huey helicopter came to rescue their unit after a particular hot engagement, my father ran toward the helicopter, hoping for the forward section of the aircraft, as there would be more room. Another soldier beat him to it, so he was forced to pile into the back with numerous other soldiers. Seconds later, as the Huey lifted off, the Viet Cong fired off a fusillade of parting shots, and that soldier who had beat him to the seat up front took a bullet to the head and was killed instantly.

God obviously had plans for my dad.

About a month and a half into my father's deployment, as he trotted through swamps on yet another search-and-destroy mission, filtering the murky waters beneath rice patties through his sock for drinking water, his team settled down for the night in a field.

Dad's platoon set up a defensive perimeter close to a wooded area. Dad felt uncomfortable with this location that the lieutenant selected. He was directed to hold a position near some trees, but as he approached that position, two other soldiers had secured it, so Dad took a position nearby for the night. Soon all hell broke loose. Dad said that the enemy was so close that he could hear them yelling and shouting. He then experienced AK-47 bullets and tracers hitting the ground all around him. Suddenly, Dad took a round to his right thigh and began bleeding profusely. It was sheer chaos. Even so, he took up an exposed position to direct his men and continued fighting despite his wound. Eventually the gunships were called in and it was quiet. Dad learned later that the two of the three soldiers killed were the ones who had taken the position that he was told to originally hold.

A medevac Huey landed to retrieve the wounded and dead. Dad was assisted by two soldiers to the chopper and literally hurled on top of fellow wounded and dead young men. Dad's only recollection was hearing the rotor of the blades above and the moaning of his wounded friends. Eight soldiers were wounded and three killed from his platoon that night.

But God had other plans.

Besides earning a Purple Heart and Army Commendation Medal with Valor, my father received something more valuable during the ambush. It's called a "million-dollar wound." The "MDW" was that rare wound that almost every American soldier who fought in Vietnam secretly prayed for. It was a wound that was just enough to take a soldier out of the fight and get him home—but not enough to cripple him for life. Now, sometimes soldiers with a MDW were put back into the field once healed—but after officials looked into my father's situation, they decided to send him home. After all, he was married and there was someone else waiting for him at home, too. *Me.*

Like many soldiers who returned home, my father rarely spoke of his time in Vietnam. But on the rare occasions my father did share, it gave me a great deal of inspiration and pride. And more importantly, it provided the foundation for my own beliefs and obligations, and my need to show bravery and persistence. Because when duty called, my father answered. He didn't run to Canada to escape or move to San Francisco to "protest" by letting his hair grow and dropping acid. Instead, he did what was asked of him, facing the evil that was present, fighting for his country, and, with much prayer and bravery, returned alive.

---

Where my dad was strict, devout, stoic, and career-oriented, my mom was quite the opposite. While she was still quite responsible, owning her own business and being successful in her own right, she was more of a romantic—impetuous and funny. She was also adventurous. In fact, before she met my father she had planned to see the world. She wanted to travel abroad and spend time in other cultures, enjoying the incredible diversity and beauty of various places. To that end, she had gotten a job as a flight attendant at Trans World Airlines (TWA), which at the time was a very glamorous position. As a side note, my mother was quite a glamourous woman. She was tall and blonde with a beautiful smile, the quintessential "California Girl." And the occupation of flight attendant was tailor-made for her. Not only would it allow her to travel for free, but it also gave her access to a world of successful businessmen who did their best to impress her. And I'm sure there were a multitude of such men who did everything they could to offer my mother everything she wanted in life.

But, again, God had other plans.

Instead of falling in love with a sultan from overseas or settling on the French Riviera, she fell in love with the guy who lived next door. The guy who wanted to be a cop. And the guy who, until he was drafted into the Army, wasn't planning on going anywhere. But that's just who my mom was and continues to be. She, perhaps, is the most giving person I have ever met. And aside from giving me the gift of life and raising me, she also gave me the greatest gift any mother could give to her child: the desire to dream big. And since she brought me to work as a stewardess in her womb until she was "too pregnant" to work anymore, she may have given me the desire to fly as well.

# 2

# Made in California

My life began on October 15, 1969, the first of three boys born to parents Sharon Ann and George "Jerry." Though I don't know the exact circumstances, I was named Daniel after a friend of my dad's. My middle name of Joseph came from the Bible, after the earthly father of Jesus. My home was in the Southern California city of Saugus, a suburb of Los Angeles. Though the city is associated with the Santa Clarita Valley, it is not as well-known as the valley of the Santa Monica Mountains, the valley that produced every caricature of California dude culture and female affectations and idiosyncrasies. The Santa Clarita Valley, rather, was a pure slice of Americana. In fact, so American is Santa Clarita that countless films and television shows have used it as a location for their shoots and continue to do so today.

I was born at a very turbulent time in our country. The Vietnam War was still raging. It was the height of the civil rights movement. And the Cold War with Russia was in full swing. But my own world was just as turbulent. While both of my parents were good to me and my brothers, they were not always good to each other, and it seemed that much of my early childhood was marked by their arguing. And while it never escalated into physical confrontation, it certainly didn't fall within what I think one would call "healthy disagreements."

Despite these disagreements, I still managed a pretty good childhood, with my mom and dad taking us on many vacations. We weren't world travelers by any means, but we traveled throughout California, from Sequoia to the desert and from ski lifts to lakes and rivers. It seemed we were always on the move in our small camper complete with a trail bike strapped to the front. While in Sequoia, my brother Steve and I would be sandwiched between my mom and dad on the little Honda Trail 90 motorcycle as we drove past the giant trees. No helmets of course. Three times a year, with our Super 8 camera in hand, the whole family would go to the desert to ride dirt bikes, shoot guns, and climb rocks. We were a family on the move, going from one adventure to another, traveling with friends, meeting relatives, and exploring all California had to offer. Looking back on those grainy Super 8 movies, I know how blessed I was to have had the parents I did. Because in the end, their interest in exposing us to the world beyond Santa Clarita laid the foundation of what would become my life goal of being a professional adventurer—call it risk-taker, if you like—and exploring all the world had to offer.

Wonderful travels aside, though, the disconnect between my mother and father continued to grow. The truth was they were just polar opposites. Theirs was a classic "kite-rock" relationship. My dad was the boulder, firmly anchored to the ground beneath him. And my mother was the whimsical flying device, who surely would have sailed whichever way the wind blew her had she not been tethered. While this relationship dynamic can work well with some couples—and even did for my parents for a period—by the time my second youngest brother was born, it just didn't seem to work for either of them anymore. My father was outgoing and friendly, but a quiet brooder who you would have to push, pull, or prod to get anything out of. My mother, on the other hand, was like a live grenade who could go zero to sixty in a flash. Our parents, they raised us well—but it seemed like everything else they did when it came to their marriage just didn't work.

Even though the arguing had become, as it does with many other families, absolutely normal in our family's private world, it eventually took its toll on me, and for much of my early childhood I found myself deeply depressed.

This culminated for me when I was a fourth grader, with memories of coming home from school, hearing the sounds of arguing from inside the house, and climbing up to the rafters in our garage to hide away and weep. To make matters worse, at this same time I had the feeling that my life had been on a pretty cruddy trajectory altogether. I was a terrible student in school, and while you could say that my home situation contributed to that, I'm not sure this would be true. In truth, I could have had the Bradys for parents as a kid and I probably still would've been a subpar student. Because the truth is, school never interested me. I didn't enjoy reading, writing, or arithmetic. History? Snoozefest. My teachers often stated that I was a very intelligent kid but was bored most of the time and didn't put forth much effort—a pretty accurate assessment if I'm being honest.

The only thing that really kept me going were the exciting family vacations, and also my little brothers, who were a blast. Don't get me wrong, my brothers and I fought all the time, and we played terrible tricks on one another, but I don't think I would have survived the first part of my life without them. I didn't know it at the time, but they were my best friends. And still are.

My childhood fortunes finally took a change for the better when I was eleven. Something happened that I shouldn't have been so happy about—but I was all the same. My parents got a divorce. In many homes, a parent's divorce can lay the groundwork for a dysfunctional adolescence, a fault line that produces tremors that radiate into the years ahead. Divorce is often pointed to as the catalyst for truancy, drug use, petty crime, and a life of troubles in general. And though I won't debate any of that, I will say that for me, my parents' divorce was an absolute blessing. It was a watershed moment in my childhood that freed me from the pain and noise of the two people who I love most in the world arguing with each other.

It was not *despite* the issues at my home when I was a child but rather *because* of them that I am incredibly grateful to both of my parents. As I mentioned, "struggle" is a part of my DNA. And as a child I got to see and witness firsthand a very real struggle that in the end resolved in an extremely healthy relationship. Both of my parents were good people. Both of my parents loved God. And they both had always been very loving and supportive toward me and my brothers—but they just couldn't make it work between themselves. I knew getting a divorce was an incredibly difficult choice for them, but I also knew that they understood their struggle was becoming my and my brothers' struggle as well. With this in mind, they did what was best for all of us.

Their perseverance was well worth it—for they both experienced that often on the other side of struggle is growth. I watched my mom and dad change after they divorced. They lived better—and they *loved better.* Not just in terms of me and my brothers when we were with them alone, but in terms of each other. Still to this day, they remain very close friends and dedicated to one another in ways I never thought possible. Once again, it was an incredible lesson to me that no matter how big and how spectacular the mess, if you put God first, He will clean it up. And He did.

As my parents settled into their new lives, peace began to return to our homes. For so long I'd felt confined and afraid to embrace the joys of life, but I suddenly found myself beginning to blossom into boyhood—which, for me, equated to unlocking the "showman" within.

The truth is, I had always been kind of a closet showman. I certainly wasn't shy around my family, but by the time I reached middle school, I had become the kid who wanted to entertain everyone. And at the time, I did it with film.

I had always loved movies. Obviously, *Star Wars* was a huge influence. So in the seventh grade, I joined the Arroyo Seco Junior High filmmakers class. I had some experience working with my father's Super 8 on our family vacations, and this was the exact same camera that we used in the film making class. We mostly toyed around with stop animation, making figurines come to life and dubbing our voices over the action. When I think back on it, had YouTube been around, I think we would've been a huge hit. However, I was even more ambitious than simply entertaining my peers. I wanted my art to be distributed to the masses. I had heard about the young director of the movie *Jaws* and how he just boldly walked onto the lot of Paramount and took over an empty office before they even hired him. And I wanted to be like that. I wanted to write and direct something big. So, the summer after seventh grade I wrote the script for a feature-length film I intended to make in the eighth grade. The story posed a very complex and intriguing question that I thought would resonate with my classmates: "What if our school was attacked by a fleet of alien invaders led by a sadistic emperor named Blacklock?"

I ran with the idea and got a $300 grant from the school. And just two months later, during a summer vacation that included a trip to Hawaii with my mom and brothers—where we threw paper airplanes out the hotel window, watched the movie *Splash* countless times, went to Pearl Harbor, and bodysurfed in the ocean (altogether one of the most memorable bonding moments I've ever had with them)—I began writing the script. On the plane flight back, I finished the screenplay. I called the opus *Galactic War One in the 31st Century*. It began like this:

> *The Emperor and Commander Blacklock with their group of soldiers have come to destroy Arroyo Seco and its teachers . . . Unless Admiral Schlund and his rebels defeat them first.*

I spent long hours during lunch and after school filming, editing, and re-editing the movie. The sheer magnitude of the task was something I'd never before experienced—a year-long project with casting calls and costumes. I was still considered a loner and didn't have many friends, and those I did have often chided me for bringing my *Star Wars* toys to school to use them in the production.

What ensued was nothing shy of mayhem as the story follows Commander Blacklock as he pretty much butchers most of the school—and with an axe no less. Thinking back on the project, it is stunning to know there was a time when adults not only allowed young students to run around filming violent set pieces—but they actually helped. Our principal, Dr. White, even took an axe to the head. Talk about commitment to my production.

After all was said and done, *Galactic War One in the 31st Century* was released during a special assembly of the entire school and staff. Compared to *Star Wars*, the title and special effects were rudimentary, but it had the intended effect on an audience of young teens. They loved it! Even today, classmates still remember the movie. It was my breakout moment in the entertainment industry. Though I'd felt at times like I'd bitten off more than I could chew, the stress invigorated me to do better. I loved attacking the goal of accomplishing something beyond all odds. I received every doubt someone tossed my way as an energy pellet to prove them wrong. In the end, I won the appreciation of my audience along with two filmmaker awards—all while maintaining a 2.7 GPA.

By the time I had finished, however, I had learned that filmmaking really wasn't for me. I had a blast doing it, but Spielberg and Lucas had nothing to fear; it just wasn't something I felt driven to do again. Nevertheless, while making the film the bug of entertaining people had bitten me. I realized I had a knack for making people smile on a larger level than just adolescent hijinks. I decided right then and there that I would pursue such a course of action in my life, beginning immediately. I put deep thought into my decision, consulted my parents, and discussed it with my friends. After all, one doesn't just become a global entertainer overnight. It takes years of commitment. It takes a disciplined path. And sometimes decades of heartbreak. But I was up to the challenge. But before I could even set off on this road to stardom, I needed a starting point.

Despite its proximity to Los Angeles, Santa Clarita wasn't exactly a breeding ground for entertainment. I found myself wondering where I could go that had international appeal and would allow me to apprentice my particular set of creative skills (which at the time weren't significant). It then occurred to me that there was such a place in Santa Clarita that would be perfect. It was an iconic entertainment center that drew people from all over the world. And it had been the springboard for some of the most successful careers in the entertainment industry, including Jay Johnson, who was the star of the television series *Soap*; ventriloquist Jeff Dunham; and, of course, one of the world's greatest daredevils, Super Dave Osborne.

I'm talking about a little place called Six Flags Magic Mountain.

It would be there where I would plant my own flag and set out to see the world. Literally.

# 3

# On Top of the World

At the age of seventeen, my ambitions began to take shape. I was the lead technician for my school's theater productions learning all I could about lighting, sound, and stage management. I stage-managed a number of productions for the school and various community events, including the 1987 inaugural ceremonies for the newly founded city of Santa Clarita. This experience opened the door for my dream job. Although the age requirement was eighteen, I managed a special interview and was given a job in Show Operations at Six Flags Magic Mountain in Valencia. In the amusement park world, working Show Operations is the end-all. It's Broadway and the Vegas Strip all in one. Where my peers at Six Flags were offered jobs in food services or ride operations, I was selected for Show Operations, and that is where I "made my bones," acting as a jack-of-all-trades for just about anything the park needed in regards to entertainment. I ran the spotlight for high-end talent. I handled lighting for the big concerts. I managed roving crews for smaller shows that were seen across the park. I even ran the sound for our dolphin and sea lion show. I particularly enjoyed working on that show and once, long after the show ended and the trainers went home, I grabbed a few fish and snuck out onto the set. I knew the show by heart from doing it so many times and would repeat the same commands that the trainers gave to the dolphins. So, after the show to the public, I did my own little private show. *(No dolphins were harmed in this production.)*

I worked hard at Six Flags and within a couple of years it paid off when they promoted me to "Arcade Technician." In the theme-park industry, this promotion was the equivalent of being called to the Majors after just starting Triple-A ball. The position came with more responsibilities, a nicer uniform, more money, a better work truck, and, most importantly, more keys to reach more parts of the park forbidden to me while in Show Operations. Needless to say, outside of management, anything maintenance-related represented the highest possible tier of the amusement park hierarchy. (Truth be told, though, I still missed Show Ops.)

My new job duties consisted of building and maintaining the games of chance in "Center Ring," fixing and maintaining hundreds of arcade games and pinball machines. It may not have sounded like much, but I treated the position as sacred as the guards outside Buckingham Palace treated theirs. One of the things that my parents had instilled in me was that no matter what I did, I would do it to the best of my abilities. And so I embraced this advice. And in just a matter of weeks I had become the best "Arcade Technician" that Six Flags Magic Mountain ever employed. As a result, it came to no surprise that I was almost immediately offered an electrician's scholarship, but I wasn't ready for a long-term career—especially as an electrician. I still had much more adventure left in me. So, I turned it down and continued working for the next few years.

I wish I could say it was ambition that drove me at Six Flags, and I suppose it was a part of my desire to achieve there. But in a larger sense, I felt like I belonged. Unlike high school, where I was a loner, at Six Flags I was respected and trusted. However, there was something else that had driven me even harder and motivated me beyond anything I ever believed I was capable of.

While working at Six Flags, I met a girl.

Shelley Alesso was a 5'9" brunette who was also from Santa Clarita. At seventeen, she was two years younger than me, but what separated us was more than just a couple of years. It was a dimension. Shelley Alesso looked like a moving statue to me. Where I may have been likable to a few people in a silly kind of way, Shelley was magnetic. People gravitated to her. The bosses liked her. The kids liked her. And damn if I didn't like her too, the very second I saw her working the Whac-A-Mole in the arcade. I had to meet her. So, I went and pretended to fix something so I could talk to her and hopefully impress her too.

My first encounter with Shelley wasn't exactly one of the "meet-cute" moments you see in films. In fact, it was almost the opposite. It was a clumsy exchange of me poking and prodding around her game in the hopes that something was broken. I hoped she might be impressed by how serious I took my job or at least mildly amused by my inherent charm, but neither was the case. In our very limited exchanges after that, she made it very clear to me that neither "entertainment" nor "amusement" was in her future plans. Her job at Six Flags was absolutely temporary and she was going to be leaving for college at the end of the summer. Even my mentioning that I had been the auteur behind the film *Galactic War One in the 31st Century* didn't seem to move the needle with her. I probably should have written Shelley Alesso off at that point, but the heart wants what the heart wants. Plus, I wasn't the type of man to be derailed from his plans if things didn't immediately go his way. I was going to find my way to Shelley's heart.

One day at the frog launch game, I finally asked her out. We went out on our first date. Shelley's mom was not excited when I showed up on my motorcycle to pick her up, but after talking with her and explaining my years of experience, she relented. It soon became your standard teenage romance, with hours upon hours spent watching TV and eating pizza together.

Just short of a year later, Shelley had graduated high school, and I was still at Six Flags—and by now, I felt like I practically owned the place. I knew everyone and everyone liked me. And while I still worked very hard and was still very good at what I did, it felt like life was passing me by and, dare I say, boring. I was getting older and all my coworkers stayed the same age. Shelley had a different path. She had started college in Riverside, roughly an hour and a half drive from where I was. I knew I couldn't compete with the distance and college men she would meet, but she held a special place in my heart and maybe, just maybe, she would still be available after college. So, we kept in touch. She inspired me to take a few classes at the local College of the Canyons.

To keep things interesting at work, I liked to push the boundaries of what Six Flags actually permitted—in other words, what exactly constituted breaking the law. This ranged from the innocuous to the dangerous. As to the former, I once changed the bathroom signs on the men's and women's restrooms. I don't know why. Call it the immature kid in me. Once I took one of the sound-effects machines, this one supplying audio for a "chicken coop game," and hid it in the stowage of concessions before turning it on. The incessant sounds of poultry cackling would drive some of my coworkers crazy. On the edgier side, I would often lead a group of impressionable new employees on an expedition into the "Old Pagoda," which at one time had been an attraction dug into the mountain at the base of the park but was eventually closed after being deemed insensitive. I used to love going in there because it was dark, cavernous, and creepy. Since my uniform and the ride mechanics' uniforms were the same, I donned a construction hard hat and scaled the most notable rollercoaster at the time: the Viper. And I did this when it was still under construction! When I was a kid, I always wanted to know what it was like to step off the roller coaster at its apex and walk on the escape ramp next to the track. Most people with a fear of heights avoid them, but for me, that feeling was exactly what made this climb so inviting. And there I was. The view was incredible and so open. I could see the Magic Mountain tower to my left, and I remember saying to it: "You're next."

When the ride opened months later, the Viper was the tallest and fastest looping coaster in the world. I signed up to be one of the extras riding the coaster for a commercial. We did roughly twenty-eight takes and after the twenty-ninth take and nearly blacking out, I tapped out. Ever since then, I haven't been able to stomach riding roller coasters. Still to this day I get easily nauseous on such rides. There went my dreams of being a fighter pilot . . .

My quasi-illegal antics continued while at Magic Mountain, and though today I'm not particularly proud of them—I'm even a bit embarrassed—it does bring a smile to my face knowing that I took so much risk just to give myself and my friends a little joy and laughter. To that end, there was one feat that nobody in the park's history had ever done nor even tried to do. And that was to scale the park's iconic 385-foot tower with its massive flagpole at its pinnacle. After my success climbing the Viper, I decided to be the first "unauthorized" person to summit the flag pole on top of Magic Mountain's Sky Tower. When I'd go there as a kid, I'd get weak knees and butterflies in my stomach standing at the observation level, but I would also wonder what it would feel like to stand on top of it outside. It both scared me and enticed me. Would I still have butterflies? I was not going to rest until I found out. In fact, not only did I decide that I was going to scale the stairway and climb the tower, but I also decided I was going to videotape it as well, documenting the entire insane adventure for all to see. Oh, and there was one other key element of this crazy idea. When I reached the very top of the ladder at the tower's peak, I was going to make a phone call.

To my credit, I did try to go through the proper protocols when I decided I wanted to climb Sky Tower. I thought the easiest, most straightforward path for me was to simply ask permission, and so I did. I approached maintenance and asked if I could change the lightbulb on top of the flagpole next time it went out. Obviously, it wasn't that simple, and I was told as much. The tower lighting was complex, highly volatile, and operated under a "strobe system." It wasn't like I was going to climb up there with a Philips 100-watt, unscrew the old one, and screw in the new one. Still, they considered reaching out to me if and when the situation came. Naturally, it didn't come quickly enough. And every day I went to work, that tower seemed to be taunting me, daring me to climb it. Throw in the fact that I needed a good reason to make my phone call, and climbing Sky Tower was something I just wanted to do. Not to mention the excitement I got dreaming about my adventurous goal.

In due course, I decided to take matters into my own hands. And to mitigate any kind of impropriety in what was clearly an unlawful, unlicensed, and unintelligent decision, I decided to memorialize my adventure for my video production class at the College of the Canyons, where I had enrolled after Shelley left for college. I thought that if I decided to make a documentary of sneaking into the park after hours, reaching the base of the tower and ascending the nearly four hundred feet of Magic Mountain's most iconic landmark—just so I could call a girl I really liked—I would be forgiven for the many laws I was breaking.

I have to say, until then, never in my life—and never since—has such a hairbrained scheme come together with such planning, precision, and success as my plot to scale Sky Tower. I and a couple friends who agreed to tag along and help rolled onto the lot after midnight, which is when they turned the park's lights off. We drove up to the security checkpoint and I flashed my employee ID to security, explaining that we were supposed to set up Christmas decorations for an event the following day. The security guard smiled and opened the gate for us. From there, I wish I could tell you that it was some incredibly cloak-and-dagger endeavor where we had to dodge further security, dismantle surveillance alarms, circumvent locked doors, and rappel up to the base of the towers. But none of that would be true. We simply snuck onto the lot, scaled the surrounding wall, and started climbing the countless stairs until we got to the top.

I'm also not going to lie about summiting the top of the tower (all of which is documented in the documentary *The Last Rocketman*). For me, reaching the top was like summiting Everest. It was everything I thought it would be—and more. The sky was crystal clear and it seemed as if I could reach out and literally touch the stars. I stood on the very top rung with the wind whistling through my hair and the blinking red light in my face, and I don't think I've ever smiled bigger or brighter. It took a moment to soak it all in. And when I did, long before Leonardo DiCaprio's Jack ever said it in *Titanic*, I thought to myself, *I'm the king of the world!*

As I stood there beaming, it was time for the *pièce de résistance*. I pulled out my cell phone and dialed the number.

She picked up.

"Hello?" she said.

"Hey, Shelley. It's me, Dan," I said.

"Oh, hey, Dan. How are you?"

"I'm great. I'm on top of the world right now. I just climbed the flagpole on top of Sky Tower—I'm calling you from there," I proudly declared.

"No way," she said. "I don't believe you."

"No. I really am," I said. "I'm even videotaping it. I'll show you when I see you."

She then paused for a moment before finally speaking.

"You're crazy, Dan."

I don't know how, but my smile grew even bigger.

Another adventure accomplished.

I was on top of the world.

The next thing I wanted to do was to leave Santa Clarita and finally go see it.

# 4

# Enter Stage Right

I had always had a long but informal relationship with stunt work. I suppose all boys do. Heck, I was riding motorcycles, shooting guns, and climbing rocks since I was four.

Who knew I was preparing for a career?

I suppose the first time I thought I could put to good use all of my boyhood training was when I was shooting my space-opera movie in junior high school. In the film's climax, I wanted to do a high fall from the roof of one of the buildings. Much to my surprise, the school approved and I was set to do it. However, my dad said no. Fathers, right? They just never let you do what you want. I did manage, though, to sneak in another high fall during a Halloween stunt show I did at a friend's ranch not too long after that. I also would do a stunt with a friend where he would hit me several times with his car in the school's parking lot. It was a great little act and always got contrasting reactions. I guess this was the main reason I loved doing stunts. I just loved the way different people responded to them. It was raw and visceral. But I also enjoyed the fact that most people shook their heads in consternation at my actions. I got fingers waved at me constantly. "Stay away from the edge!" "Don't do that!" "You're going to *hurt* yourself!"—et cetera. Don't get me wrong, they were mostly right. I probably did take it too far. And, naturally, I would indeed end up hurting myself.

But I had a blast doing it.

Along with my friend Dave Kilde (who would later rescue me from a life-threatening crash), we would rent sports cars and practice stunt driving in empty parking lots or on vacant land for hours on end. We would practice jumping from one car to the other, getting hit and dragged, and leaping from a car off the side of bridge into water below. We even set ourselves on fire. For real. Thinking back on it, my guardian angel certainly had his hands full with me—it's simply a miracle we didn't kill ourselves ten times over.

While I'm sure they may have existed, it never occurred to me to search for a "stunt school." And I imagine even had I gone, I would've just been doing the same kind of stuff Dave and I were doing in our spare time. We didn't consider ourselves daredevils; we were training to be stunt professionals. Either way, there wasn't any kind of certification to start in the field; you just needed some experience and the willingness to risk yourself. I had both. The other thing you needed was a lead for some potential work. And at the age of twenty, I got that too when the company that did the high-diving show at Magic Mountain was looking for stuntmen for a new show they had in Virginia. I applied and obtained the position of stuntman with the understanding that at first, I was just going to be in the "actor" role, but once I got there, I learned all the stunts and did everything else.

Water Country USA, the "Virginia water park" gig, was my first semi-professional foray into stunt work. Since I was still learning on the fly, I was shown new techniques on how to do much of the same things I was already doing but just learned how to do them the right way. Like how to be set on fire without actually burning myself. Or how to fall off a thirty-foot platform without breaking your neck—and making it look real. Overall, it was a fantastic experience. But when the show was over, I returned to California with no money in my pocket, no degree to fall back on, and no direction in life. I thought about returning to school. I had some courses at the College of the Canyons under my belt, but everything I wanted to do, or thought I *could* do, required a comprehensive curriculum of study that would take me years to achieve. And I just didn't have the patience or the money. I thought and prayed on it, but nothing ever came to mind.

Then one day something caught my attention. I was driving—I don't remember where I was going—and minding my own business when suddenly lights appeared in my rearview along with the ear-splitting sound of a siren. I pulled over as you're supposed to and then watched as an ambulance whizzed by on its way to the scene of an accident or something else. It's one of those things that I had probably seen a hundred times in my life but never thought twice about it. But this time it gave me pause. I got to thinking, hey, that might be a pretty good job. I'd get to drive fast and put on a siren just like my dad. I began imagining the adventure of responding to unknown situations. And I'd be helping people, too. So, I looked into it and, lo and behold, I discovered I could get my certificate as an EMT in just one semester.

And just like that, I had a new career.

---

In 1994, after studying and earning the proper credentials, I was officially hired as an emergency medical technician in the state of California, working the Palmdale/Lancaster area of northern Los Angeles County. Though the training was demanding and comprehensive, there was nothing that could have fully prepared me for what I was really about to experience.

First off, my shifts would be forty-eight hours on, forty-eight hours off. I didn't even know that was legal at the time, but it was similar to being a firefighter. The station we worked out of was actually very nice and became a second home to me. Secondly, I had no idea how much driving was involved. Until I had started my job as an EMT, my preconceptions were based on what I had seen in movies or the old television show *Emergency*. I envisioned myself administering CPR to people on the brink of death. Or rushing them to the hospital where I would have to burst through the doors of the emergency room to get my patient into the right hands. Don't get me wrong, there would be plenty of that. But most of my time spent as an EMT was in the ambulance transferring a patient from one hospital to another, when we weren't running 911 calls. While I learned this was typical of most EMTs, the area I was assigned to cover was particularly large. In fact, it was so large that we would often have a thirty-to-forty-five-minute response time to a crash or injured person. Throw in the fact that this was before GPS and iPhones. All we had were the

Thomas Guide paper maps to navigate with—tough to work with while you're splitting through traffic on the way to the hospital. So, while the station may have been my second home, the ambulance was basically my bedroom.

One of the most striking things about the job I was soon to discover was not just the fragility of life, but the randomness of death. The drunk driver lives and the family of four are killed. As a young man who had always lived his life with much daring-do, I had not thought about death all that much or even really thought it possible; I was seemingly invincible. Also, being a believer, I almost thought I was impervious to it. Spiritually, I was right. With my faith in Christ, I would never die. But technically, a physical death could have been calling for me (or you) at any time. While working as an EMT I saw this firsthand and it became incredible to me how close to death life truly is. I remember on one occasion we rushed to a crash site where the vehicle went off the side of the road on a small bridge. The bridge's guardrail had smashed through the front passenger windshield and went straight out the back window. There was a passenger seated in the car, and, by all rights, she should have been killed instantly. However, she had been sleeping with her seat laid back at the time of the accident and the guardrail went over her head. She survived without a scratch. Other times, those at the scene of an accident weren't so blessed. (I wouldn't call them lucky.) On one such occasion we received a call to a seemingly minor crash that involved a motorcycle and a school bus. Once we were there, it didn't seem like much. It wasn't like the motorcycle was trashed, and its rider was still in one piece. There was no blood. He was wearing his helmet but apparently had been knocked unconscious. But once we got a closer look at the rider, it was clear that he could have been declared dead on the scene. (Head injuries were like that sometimes. I had seen the heads of some accident victims split wide open with enough blood to paint the sidewalk and some of them could still carry on a full conversation.) Due to the presence of all the children on the bus, we were instructed to put the motorcyclist in the back of the ambulance and to try to revive him. We tried to pump oxygen into his lungs and do CPR in the hope that it might. But in the end, when God calls—it's your time.

To be honest, while I never felt being an EMT was my ultimate calling in life, I do think it was a job that God wanted me to experience. It allowed me to obtain skills that I could use throughout my entire life. And more important than the tangible skills I learned like CPR or scuba diving was what I learned about myself. There's something incredibly moving about being so near the fabric of life; it made it impossible not to believe that God had a hand in everything I was witness to—even the tragedies. One of the moments that hits home for me in this respect happened shortly after I was transferred to a new division in the Los Angeles Basin. The area wasn't nearly as big as the Palmdale/Lancaster territory, but it was far more diverse, populated and dangerous. One of the neighborhoods we covered was Compton, which has long held a reputation for being a violent, gang-infested area. I remember one time coming back from a call in a particularly rough part of that city and when we pulled up to a stoplight and a gang member's car pulled up alongside of us. As I looked over, the passenger reached up his shirt and revealed that he was carrying a firearm. He was just a kid, maybe twenty, and maybe he was just looking for a reaction. The only response I had was to brandish my stethoscope to show I was armed too. We then just stared at each other for an odd but tense moment. On the surface, the two of us could not have been more unalike. I was also in my twenties, blond-haired, blue-eyed, and, by appearances, well-off. He was Hispanic, with brown eyes and short, dark hair covered by a bandana, and, by appearances, poor. But there was an understanding in that moment. An understanding that while we may have both come from very different places, there was a common spirit that we shared: a spirit of dedication to our cause, one that informed us that we were still both connected in some way through our magnificent Creator. The light changed and both of our vehicles took off, going our separate ways.

I dealt with such a wide variety of situations as an EMT. Sometimes it was a call about a "5150" psych patient who hadn't taken their medication and was causing all sorts of problems, forcing us to restrain them. Sometimes it was a simple "Code 2 transfer," which meant we were just a shuttle for a patient from one hospital to the next. And on very rare occasions it was a bizarre call altogether. One time we went to a home to pick up a middle-aged woman who was not feeling well and disoriented. Entering the home, we saw her lying on the couch. When I pulled away the blanket she had a .38 revolver in her hand. I asked, "What's that for?" She stated, "In case anyone breaks in." This delusional woman could have easily shot us when we knocked on the door or when I approached her. Luckily, I have a very friendly voice.

Of all the various 911s I went on, my most dreaded calls came from convalescent homes. Even before I ever stepped in one, I never liked convalescent homes. They always struck me as super-depressing, and like most people, I never really knew what to say or do. In my understanding, these were simply places where old people were sent to die. Well, they didn't disappoint. While some homes were actually nicer than I had imagined, clean and with plenty of staff and activities, others were a nightmare. Some of the lower-rated ones were unkempt. They smelled like fecal matter and urine. And cries for help echoed through their halls with an unending parade of flashing lights from "nurse call" lights outside residents' rooms going unanswered. It was in these places that my passion for being an EMT deteriorated. I could handle the trauma of accidents and psych patients and even death. But I could not stomach despair, and it was the convalescent calls that broke me. Not because the people there were sick or suffering but because they were *alone.* To make matters worse, our presence at convalescent homes wasn't always the best received. It took me a while to figure out why, but one time when we were called to a home and rushed in to check on the resident I heard someone say, "The EMTs just arrived with the meat wagon." He was talking about us. I then realized that every time we walked into a convalescent home, everyone there knew something bad must've happened. All of these people were at the end of their rope. Once I learned this, I did my best to be as kind as I could while I was there. I learned what to say and do. It would only make sense that I would eventually receive my biggest life lesson while responding to a call from one of these homes.

One day my partner and I got a generic call for a "sick woman" at a home in the San Fernando Valley. We rushed over there with a lot of urgency and bravado per usual, storming into the place like heroes. We had gone on a number of these calls before and I was expecting to see some woman who was on the brink of death, but was surprised to find the woman wasn't that old, and, to be honest, not all that sickly. All vitals normal. She had good skin color, a thick head of hair, and even seemed to have her wits about her. But she was alone. Her only companion was the television that sat in front of her chair, an oxygen tank, and a large bowl of cigarette butts on the stand next to her. We did a quick examination of her, asked her the perfunctory questions of the trade, and when we were done it had been pretty clear that she was fine. No ailments. No pain. And no signs of anything pending. Once she was cleared, my partner was packing up when, to his surprise, I sat next to the woman and put my arm over her shoulder.

"Sweet pea," I said to her. "Are you just lonely?"

She hesitated a moment before breaking down in tears. I knew what the answer was.

"Do you need a hug?" I asked.

She said, "Yes."

And we then embraced.

I remember at the time thinking about how good that hug must have felt for her; that she had been so hungry for human connection that she was willing to call an ambulance for it. But the truth of that embrace was that I felt *helpless.* And in that moment, I realized that most of the pain I would ever see in people was something even the best of medics could never help alleviate. I know it may sound insignificant, but that little encounter with that older woman changed my life. After four years of running 911 and non-emergency calls in the L.A. Basin, I realized I could not continue being an EMT. I lacked the emotional stamina it took to endure the job any longer. So, I did what I usually do. I talked to a professional counselor; I prayed on it. And I decided that I had to quit, giving up a full-time job with security, benefits, the whole deal, and just trusted that God would open another door for me.

As it would happen, He didn't open a door.

He opened a window.

# 5

# Waiting for the Call

I had learned about "set medics" through my buddy Dave Kilde while visiting him on set. They were the EMTs and paramedics who worked on movie and television sets in the event someone got hurt. I know that sounds kind of cool, but to me it sounded boring. I wanted to be in an ambulance and speed around the city meeting and helping the public. I didn't want to be on the set of a show just in case some actor or actress got light-headed. However, the idea of doing stunts for a living still appealed to me a great deal, and I thought if I started working on set it would give me a chance to be around the entertainment business and meet stunt coordinators. It didn't hurt that set medics paid really well, too. And I did get some stunt opportunities, thanks to my devious plan to hustle stunt coordinators on set.

Being a set medic wasn't nearly as boring as I thought it would be. But it was close. Especially coming from my previous job where we sped to accidents and faced life-or-death situations several times a day. It made me feel guilty, but I was always hoping something terrible would happen on set. Of course, I didn't want anyone to get hurt, but I was admittedly just always waiting for someone to scream in panic, "MEDIC!" Unfortunately, it rarely came. The set medic is probably the only person on set that the producer *didn't* want to work.

The job was slow as I did my rounds making sure everyone was hydrated and didn't need anything else—but it did have its moments. One time, I was working on a set where a construction worker was cutting a two-by-four with a SKIL saw—and continued cutting straight into his leg. The laceration was about four inches deep but, thankfully, the saw blade missed all the vital blood vessels. Still, it was a pretty grisly accident. There was blood everywhere and the rest of the set was pretty panicked. But the worker was a tough Marine who didn't make a fuss about it at all. He didn't blink through the whole ordeal, in fact, and we conversed rather casually as I bandaged him up before he was driven to the hospital.

Eventually, I became accustomed to the rhythm of being a set medic and came to really appreciate being behind the scenes of a film. While my presence was purely an insurance policy, it gave me a chance to fully value the hard work and passion that goes into entertainment. I couldn't help but admire the players, everyone from the creative team to the production grips to the assistants who worked the craft-service table. Like me, they all shared a dream. But unlike me, they were living theirs out. I was just watching.

Until one day I received a call from Dave Kilde. He and I had almost killed ourselves a hundred times trying to learn how to be stuntmen, and in the six years since, Dave had begun to carve himself a nice little niche in the stunt world within motion pictures. Dave did a number of high-profile stunts, doubling John Travolta in *Swordfish* and working on the Indiana Jones franchise as well as *The Matrix*. It wasn't surprising. Not only did Dave work hard at his craft, he worked just as hard at marketing himself—and he was terrific at both. Dave and I even worked on a low-budget film together, coordinated by our mutual friend Hunter Brown. We played SWAT officers and rappelled off a rooftop shooting guns as we descended the brick wall.

Anyway, Dave had been called to produce a stunt show in Taiwan for six months. It was one of those "bread and butter" gigs that all entry-level stunt coordinators chase after, but as Dave's career had begun to take off, he wanted to put his energies into film and television. (This decision was yet another stroke of genius for Dave because by the time he would reach thirty, he would be one of the hottest stuntmen in all of Hollywood.) So he asked me if I wanted to help produce the show. It would be a real job in the field I wanted. Had I ever produced a full show with stunts? he'd asked. Clearly, he had missed the hype of *Galactic War One in the 31st Century*. Did I know anything about Taiwan? Nope. To be honest, I didn't even know where it was. After reviewing the budget, Dave decided it best to continue his movie career and gave me his blessing to pursue the contract on my own. Where Dave would excel in the movie business, I would excel in the live stunt show industry.

A month later I was on a plane to Taipei.

Though I'd traveled the U.S. a bit—except for one trip to Tijuana that we won't talk about—I had never been out of the country. The Leofoo Village Theme Park is in Guanxi, Hsinchu County, Taiwan. The park had originally been a wildlife reserve with tigers and rhinos and all sorts of other wild animals, but they changed it to strictly an amusement park in 1989. I don't know what they did with all the animals. And while I was there, the thought would occasionally cross my mind that I would come across some crazed boar or something. It was just another thing to worry about. My greater concern was to do the job I was hired for—a job I'd never done before.

Producing stunt shows isn't exactly something they teach you in school, so I figured learning by doing was the only way to go. As the type of guy who jumps in with both feet first, *then* learns to swim, I had an abundance of confidence that I could achieve anything I'd set my mind to. Like anything else, producing the stunts was just a matter of solving problems. I needed to write a script, hire a crew, incorporate the existing equipment, and add a few more pieces. The agents helped me with the Taiwanese police and local authorities to import the guns, ammunition, and explosives.

It turned out that one of the other companies bidding on the Taiwan job was the same production company that had produced that low-budget film Dave and I had worked on; and Hunter Brown just happened to be the previous stunt coordinator at the Leofoo Village Theme Park (which I didn't know at the time). The producers invited me to the office to give me a copy of the finished movie, but in truth they were there to convince me to drop out of the Taiwan bidding so they had no competition. "You're not experienced enough," they told me. "It's too complicated." The comment that irked me the most was: "Drop your bid and come in with us—we'll give you something to do on it."

I was pissed. I called my Taiwan agent and told them that I didn't care what the budget was, I wanted this gig. I would show them. We soon won the bid, so I guess the people who mattered could see that we were up to the challenge. I gathered a good team and packed as much stunts and action as we could into thirty minutes. One of the things that I did with my show that I am particularly proud of, was that I created an "inclusive" story. I know that's kind of a buzzword for this current generation, but at the time, women were rarely used in stunt shows, especially in Taiwan. If they were used at all, it was usually for set dressing or to play the damsel in distress. So I made it a point to make a woman the hero. I didn't do this to make some kind of statement, but I just thought it would be a refreshing angle to the show. I also brought in bigger stunts and greater effects than the previous companies did in the past. I ended up hiring a team of stunt people: four men, two women. The show would include a massive propane explosion and a fifty-foot pendulum swing for the women. Yes, it took a bigger chunk out of my budget, but I really wanted the audience to come away from our show thrilled—and it worked. Audience response was tremendous. In fact, so overwhelmingly positive were the crowds that the park renewed our contract for an additional six months.

At the time, I was only twenty-seven years old and one of the youngest stunt coordinators on the live-show circuit. I was also making more money than I had ever made in my life with a $40,000 annual salary. Sitting in the stands one day, watching my team rehearse, playing around with staff, I had a transcendental realization: *Wow, I put all this together.* It was the peak of my early adult life and something I'll never forget. Best yet, one of the producers from that competing production company visited to see the show. Afterwards he told me I'd done a good job and added lots of stuff that really enhanced the performance. Vindication!

But while the show was a huge success for me, the feeling of pride for having accomplished what I did was also fleeting. Leofoo Village was my first real business endeavor, and being so new to producing, coordinating, and wearing so many hats, it was a real grind. In fact, midway through the second season, things began to get particularly rough for me. You often hear or read about members of bands being on the road for too long, or how resentment can fester among people who have worked together closely for too long. This is something I never understood. I thought if you love something, you could just keep doing it. Like, forever. Well, as it turned out, "forever" was only about nine months for me. That's a long time to be with people who, even if professional, are not your family, and animosities and frustrations are certain to take hold. I didn't feel welcomed. I was the boss, and a green boss at that. In the end, "Concrete," a stuntman on my team who'd been my right-hand man throughout the Taiwan engagement, circumvented my authority and took control of the project. I don't know if it was because I was doing poorly or if it was personal, but regardless, I let it happen. It was a sad but very important life and leadership lesson on how to lead a team of people with more experience than me, how to maintain control of a dicey situation, and how to balance friendship and leadership.

I could have fought that coup, but I didn't. The truth is, as long as I was paid, I didn't care at that point. I missed home. I missed my family. Heck, I even missed set medic jobs. But I did vow never to let that happen to me again.

---

It was a culture shock returning to the Santa Clarita Valley. I have to say, as wonderful as the experience overseas was, I did not quite "embrace" Taiwanese culture. In fact, I struggled with it quite a bit. Obviously, there was a great language barrier and the people themselves were very kind and polite. But they were not particularly expressive. People often take for granted the unbridled individualism of American culture. It can be loud, overwhelming, even abrasive. But you can't say it's boring. I found Taiwanese culture to be very staid. It was also secular and enforced strict business and social laws. I always felt like I was walking on eggshells during the performance. The agent would be fined if we missed a stunt, misbehaved, or even went to see one of the other shows. Staff watched every show with a checklist to make sure everything was performed correctly. It was tyrannical. But I wrote in my contract that my team would not face any fines pertaining to rejected stunts. I believed it a necessity that if one of my stuntmen or stuntwomen didn't feel comfortable doing a stunt, they should not be faced with the threat of not getting paid. The key to survival in stunt work is if something doesn't feel right, don't do it!

Then there was *the food.* With my deepest apologies to Taiwanese cuisine, it was terrible. We'd driven by street markets with pigs and ducks hanging in the open-air market, and at every meal I wondered if that was what I was eating. I even asked a Taiwanese coworker if I ever ate dog and they said, "Maybe, you never know." With reassurances such as that, I eventually ended up eating at McDonalds three times a day. Between stress and diet, I lost so much weight that I ended up at 145 pounds. Also, in case you were wondering, the lodging wasn't exactly the Ritz-Carlton, either. We were put up in a six-story flat with each person having their own five-hundred-square-foot floor with one bathroom to share. Returning home to my comfortable bed, familiar food, and family was a welcome relief and a reminder of how lucky I had always been. I felt guilty as I slept in a warm, comfortable bed while my team was toiling "in the field."

With Leofoo on my résumé now but no other opportunities to produce a show of my own, I was hired to do an Indiana Jones–style stunt show in Holland the following year. It was the same company that I worked for in Virginia. Having recovered from my time in Taiwan and having no other prospects, I was ready for another adventure, and this time I was happy to find one somewhere more pleasant. As stunt shows went, this was a great career move. This time, I'd be strictly performing not producing. It was a great addition to my growing résumé. While I was there, I took some time off to visit Paris and did something else I had always wanted to do, which, if you could guess, was also something not too bright: I ran with the bulls in Pamplona, Spain. It is an event that has killed over a dozen people over the years and injures at least fifty to a hundred people annually. And where most people have seen the highlights of this tradition and have asked themselves if the runners are out of their minds, I saw highlights of it and said to myself, *I have to do that!* So I went and checked it off my bucket list with my cousin Stevie, a chemical engineer who was working in Belgium at the time.

The show in Holland was much more enjoyable than the one in Taiwan, and the food, language, and culture was admittedly much more agreeable to me. Without the burden of producing and coordinating and all the other responsibilities of a producer, I was allowed to simply do what I do best: perform. And as a cherry on top of the gig, at the end of the season my father flew out and we backpacked throughout Europe like a couple of college grads, staying in hostels and taking trains. My father had actually never been out of the country except for Vietnam, so it was a big step for him to be in another foreign land. He would only come if I rented a car so we could drive. But for those who travel Europe, you know it's the opposite of America; public transportation is the best mode of transportation. So, I lied and told him I had rented a car. Once he arrived it was too late for him to gripe (though he did). But after a few days he agreed with me. We went to Rome, Paris, and even the Vatican. Being a devout Catholic, the Vatican leg of the trip was a dream come true for him. It was one of the greatest bonding moments I've ever had with my dad, one hell of an adventure, something both of us look back on with great admiration.

Yet traveling together like a couple of college grads brings its own challenges, such as watching each other's back on the subway and sharing a hostel room with strangers. We found ourselves having to truly rely on one another in a different land with a different culture and unfamiliar risks. But from struggle comes the best kind of closeness: fellowship, a mutual quest for a desired goal, something that not all families and even friends get to experience.

Returning home from Europe in 1998, I was looking at a shift in my career to full-time stunts. And with my experience in theme parks and working abroad, I was starting to have the experience to back it up. Feeling some momentum and eager to sell another stunt show, I went to attend the International Association of Amusement Parks and Attractions Expo in Dallas, Texas. IAAPA is an annual trade show of industry experts from amusement parks, hotels and resorts, aquariums, and just about any other venue that incorporates large-scale productions into their entertainment. But the show floor also fills with thousands of exhibitors hawking everything from food and beverage to games and arcade to operations services to rides and, of course, show productions. Though I didn't have a booth, a business card, or anything else with which to represent myself, I went in the hopes of making a divine connection.

One of my favorite things about the IAAPA was indeed the show floor. I just loved walking around, taking a peek at all of the booths. Some were low-level manufacturers who offered cheap trinkets as arcade prizes. Some were pitching new games or rides. There were products too, like new go-karts and top-of-the-line laser guns available to order. There were displays for inflatables and even exhibitions for new attractions (I remember one called "Ninja Jump," which was basically an outdoor gym on steroids). But as I meandered around the show floor, taking it all in, something grabbed my attention. It was a small booth that had something strange and spectacular on display.

It looked like a jet pack, similar to the one Boba Fett wore in *The Empire Strikes Back*. But it was real. Something you could touch. Something you could wear and fly. It resembled an art piece from the Buck Rodgers era with its stainless-steel tanks, precisely machined handles, and compact size.

But what really caught my attention, as if love at first sight, was the video of the pilot flying effortlessly through the air. Zooming fast, sweeping turns, hovering. It wasn't just powerful, but graceful too.

Then there were all the different countries, celebrities, and venues whose presence this "jet pack" graced. It was clear this technology produced the *crème de la crème* of live-action stunt performances.

Standing in front of the booth was a beautiful woman a few years older than I with long dark hair. She carried a wide, inviting smile. And confidence, most of all was the confidence. I walked up to her.

"Hi, I'm Dan Schlund," I said, my eyes riveted on the jet pack.

It looked like it was built just for me.

"I'm a stuntman and I've never seen anything like this before."

"I'm Sheri Gibson," she said.

And then she said the words that changed my life.

"And this is the 'Rocketbelt.'"

I must have stayed at the Rocketbelt booth for three hours talking to Mrs. Gibson. As we spoke, she shared a brief history of the Rocketbelt and how her husband, Kinnie Gibson, had been a pioneer in the industry. She highlighted the promotional video of some of the shows Kinnie had done and I was just in awe. It was adrenaline at first sight. I saw him flying around the Sphinx in Egypt, zipping over the Superbowl, hovering over parades. And as I watched him, it seemed as if everything I had ever done in my life— the filmmaking, the training, the job at Six Flags, the medical work, the stunt production abroad—had all coalesced in one singular moment. *This is what I was meant to do.*

It took every ounce of my restraint to not just stop talking and simply beg Sheri Gibson, right there on the spot, to introduce me to her husband so that I might have a chance to fly that Rocketbelt. But I kept my cool. I listened. Asked questions. And I shared about myself too: where I had worked, what I had done. (And tried to pour as much "Schlund charm" on her as I could muster.) And at the end of our conversation, she surprised me with something I truly wasn't expecting.

"Well, Dan. I think I'm going to introduce you to my husband, Kinnie. I think you'd make a pretty good pilot."

---

Kinnie Gibson began his career as a balloonist, specializing in "aerial stunts." A native of Texas, he befriended Chuck Norris and became his exclusive stunt double throughout the actor's career, winning countless awards for the show *Fall Guy*. But he also worked on dozens of other shows too, including *The A-Team*, *Knight Rider*, *CHiPs* and most notably *Walker, Texas Ranger*. Besides being a stunt legend Kinnie was also the "Rocketman," a persona he created as the sole owner and proprietor of the aviation world's only functional Rocketbelt. (It's sometimes referred to as a jet pack, though it's technically different. A jet pack is propelled by a jet engine using jet fuel. The Rocketbelt uses a rocket engine and produces thrust by forcing propellant into a catalyst, similar to what is used in the space shuttle and satellites to maneuver in outer space. There were no Rocketbelts *or* jet packs in existence at this time, apart from Kinnie's.)

The Rocketbelt, I had learned, had long been the Rosetta stone in the subculture of self-propelled flight. Although the idea of the jet pack was very much in the consciousness of American pop culture—in everything from *Buck Rodgers* to *Star Wars*—the truth was, no such belt was ever created that was actually functional or practical. Bell Aerospace created the technology over the late '50s and early '60s for the U.S. Army, but even the best they could produce was a heavy, cumbersome device that could only fly for about twenty-one seconds at a time. Kinnie widened that to thirty seconds. Oh, and they were dangerous as hell, too. Putting on a Rocketbelt was literally strapping a ginormous bottle rocket to your back. And not only did the pilot run the risk of crashing or burning themselves to cinders, the belts were nearly impossible to pilot. The thrust is so violent that without precise placement of the control arms, it could easily knock you over, fling you backwards, or throw you sideways into a wall. If you didn't train attached to a safety cable, you didn't live long. On the plus side, a rocket engine is much safer than a jet engine as the latter has a great many moving parts, any one of which could fail. The Rocketbelt engine only had one moving part, the throttle valve. This controlled how much propellant you forced into the catalyst. This simplicity actually helped me feel comfortable flying a hundred feet in the air. The Rocketbelt is truly a reliable and sturdy device.

Still, you have to learn to pilot it, and that is no small task. There has always been a huge swath of pilots and pilot-wannabes who have tried to "crack the code" of the Rocketbelt. Not just because the dream of flight has been ingrained into the human condition since the dawn of man, but whoever could figure out how to make a functional jet pack—nonetheless fly it—could become pretty rich in doing so. And Kinnie Gibson had done just that.

I'm not generally a fanboy when it comes to "celebrities" (except for George Lucas). The people I've always most admired have been my parents. But I was incredibly nervous prior to meeting with Kinnie. Not only did I admire what he accomplished, but his reputation was outstanding. He was also one of the few guys in that field who could "make or break" you. Over the course of my brief foray into the entertainment industry, I discovered that life-altering opportunities were few and far between—and few of those ever panned out anyway. So while I was encouraged that I seemed to win over Sheri, I imagined Kinnie would be a much more difficult nut to crack.

And I was right.

Kinnie Gibson was not exactly Tickle Me Elmo. He was confident, well-built, quiet, and intimidating, and his default expression was akin to a thousand-yard stare. He was a serious guy. However, my father was a pretty serious guy too, and I certainly knew that personality. I figured with Kinnie, it would be the same, which is to say I needed to be humble and would have to listen more than I spoke. And so that's exactly what I did.

I ended up spending the entire evening with Kinnie Gibson and his family. On the way to dinner, I was riding in the back of his van with his children Westly and Lacy. Westly was only about ten years old and asked me a curious question for his age: "Have you been saved?" Growing up Catholic and being "confirmed," I believed I was and explained to him that, yes, I believed in Jesus and followed him. And it wasn't just a ploy to gain favor.

I had a wonderful but nerve-racking dinner with the family, and afterwards Kinnie and I just sat around and talked for about two hours before they dropped me off at my cheap motel. As I had hoped, as the evening progressed I had earned my respect with Kinnie, and he began to lower his guard with me, asking me questions about my life and what I had planned to do. I was completely candid about my desires to continue stunt work, but I also emphatically shared my enthusiasm to apprentice with him in any way that would make me a part of his team. I told him that I would do whatever it took and that I would work harder than anybody he had employed. And I went on, passionately explaining how I fit perfectly into the Rocketman culture he had created. That culture being an All-American Hero. And how my experience in international shows had made me a fearless performer. And how I envisioned the Rocketbelt performances eventually becoming one of the iconic showstopping finales for the biggest events in the world. I let it all out. It was probably the first, and last, time I had ever pushed all of my cards in. But in that moment, I could not have been more excited or self-assured that becoming a Rocketman was my destiny.

By the end of the night I was high on adrenaline, absolutely overjoyed by our meeting. I was also quite sure that I had made an impression—especially after Kinnie caught me on my way out, pulled me in, thanked me, and said, "Well, we are looking for a new pilot and will keep you in mind."

Less than I wanted, but more than I hoped for. We shook hands. Traded information. And I flew back to California.

I never heard from him again.

# PART TWO

# LIFTOFF, INTERRUPTED

"For I know the plans I have for you," declares the LORD,
"plans to prosper you and not to harm you,
plans to give you hope and a future."
—Jeremiah 29:11

# 6

# The Call

You can only hold your breath for so long. And even though I left Texas under the impression that Kinnie Gibson would be calling me any moment, after a couple of months it was clear that Kinnie's call wasn't going to come any time soon—if it came at all. Oh, but it didn't stop me from badgering him every other week for two years, checking in and keeping him up to date with what I was doing. But most of the time I just ended up talking with Sheri, who was pretty much screening his calls. I'm not going to say I wasn't hurt at the time. At twenty-nine, I was already a man who was accustomed to getting what he wanted. But I also wasn't raised to wallow in self-pity or pine away at impossible dreams. My father had survived Vietnam. And my mother taught me persistence. Both taught me to have faith and work hard and that God would sort out the rest. And thus far in my life, they had been right. So instead of falling into a deep depression over what might have been, I decided to dive fully into stunt work. My plan was that I would work so hard and get so good at my craft, Kinnie Gibson would have to call me eventually. In the meantime, after finishing my contract in Holland, the company signed me to another contract at Six Flags Marine World in Vallejo,

California. As its name suggested, its attractions were more water-oriented than other parks.

Marine World ended up being one of the best experiences of my life, and it was exactly what I needed at the time. Since my last Six Flags job fixing arcade games in Santa Clarita, I'd grown up. I was a man now, so this time, there was no high jinks with other departments. There was no scaling of rides. And there was nothing close to those old on-shift shenanigans with coworkers. And the thing was, I didn't even miss any of it—well, maybe a little, but I guess I had matured finally and the new job supplied plenty of action and adventure on its own.

Like my first show in Virginia, I started the job as lowest man on the totem pole, assigned the least amount of the easiest stunts: fights and minor falls. I was never picked to do the big, thrilling stunts. At the end of the day, stunt work isn't unlike any other job in corporate America; those with experience, longer tenure, or a better résumé will always come first. It didn't matter that I was younger or that I had cultivated a better persona as a stuntman. I was the new guy and still a bit of a loner, and the new guys stayed at the bottom of the pecking order—that is, until one of those opportunities came around where management incredibly intervenes and demands that the stunt person is assigned a more prestigious position. Or . . . until someone makes a mistake.

One day during our training, one of our primary stuntmen was practicing a high fall off a huge thirty-foot statue of a fire-breathing cobra. It was the show's finale and undeniably its best stunt. The stuntman was positioned at the crown of the snakehead before a stream of fire that blasted out of its mouth. It always drew gasps from the crowd. It was also a fall I had probably done a thousand times, minus the fire. But that's the thing about stunt work. It doesn't matter how many times you've done it. It's the stuntmen with the most seniority who get the best stunt roles, and I have to admit, there's good reason for it: *Every stunt is different*, even the ones that are the same by all appearances, and with more experience comes more ability to handle the unexpected. And it's not only each stunt that's different—every stuntperson is distinct from every other stuntperson. Our time-sense constantly fluctuates and even if it's just a beat, give or take, that time fluctuation affects the timing and rhythm of a fall. Also, environment affects stunts as well. Indoor stunts are very much different from outdoor stunts. There's wind sometimes. There's the glare of the sun. Or the hot or cold environment; we sweat and we shiver.

Ultimately, everything in stunt work is timing, and to pull off a more ambitious set piece, the timing has to be akin to a Swiss watch.

In this particular case, we didn't have a good landing pad—it was very stiff and even a slight error in landing was going to be painful. And here's where timing came in: On this particular high-fall practice, the stuntman over-rotated. As a result, instead of landing on his back, he landed on his legs, which snapped upwards, bringing his knees up and into his face. His nose shattered and he broke the orbital bone in one of his eyes. Being an EMT, I knew exactly what to do and provided urgent medical care until the helicopter came to fly him off.

The good news: The stuntman, except for a few facial scars, was going to be okay. In fact, as awful as the injury sounded and looked, in the stunt world it was just an occupational hazard. The show must go on.

The better news? The show now needed someone to fill in for him. Obviously, there was some politics and lobbying involved. Imagine the lead of a movie dropping out and how many suitable actors would come forward to pitch themselves about how they could fill the role. However, after such a horrific accident, almost every stuntman we had shied away from making their pitch to the director and stunt coordinator.

Except me.

They certainly could have picked one of the more senior stuntmen, but no one else had the experience I had in high falls. Nor did they want to follow in his footsteps. They also entertained the idea of simply cutting the stunt from the show altogether. But I convinced them that not only was the stunt necessary for the show, but that I was the right performer to pull it off. This latter was quite the claim. Because the truth was . . . I had never done a fall to such an unforgiving landing pad. I had certainly done falls of the same height in Virginia and at the amusement park Walibi Flevo (now known as Walibi Holland) in the Netherlands. But not anything with *fire that would blast in your face* on your way down if your timing was off. This was a variable I had definitely never encountered.

The show's director and stunt coordinator studied me after my pitch. Then they called me out.

"Okay," the stunt coordinator said. "If you feel safe, do it now. In front of everyone."

---

The climb is the easiest part. I had been climbing things my entire life, everything from trees to rocks and, yes, towers. Climbing something incredibly high and standing on the edge with no safety railing was as second nature to me as walking. But as I began to ascend the ladder of the faux rock building that led to the top of the statue, for some reason I began to doubt myself. Right before I had begun the climb, in fact, the stunt coordinator had pulled me aside for a second time, concerned.

"Dan, are you sure you can do this?" he asked.

"I got this," I said confidently. And just started climbing. But as I did, the weight of my hubris began to sink in. I then realized that I had put the team in a pretty rough position. The team had already lost one of their top performers. If I got hurt or injured trying the same fall on the same day, their jobs would possibly be on the line. Of course there was concern, especially after such a critical injury. And what would it do to the morale of the other stunt workers? On the other hand, it's critical that the last stunt be a good stunt for the morale of the team. If not, their day would go from bad to worse and the park might even cancel the show, leaving us all out of work. I thought for a moment. The stunt wasn't about me. It was about the show. It was about the team. And it was about the park. *Now I had to make the fall.*

Standing at the crown of the fire-breathing snake, an uncertain feeling washed over me. Not because I didn't think I could do it but because the way the opportunity had dropped into my lap and the way I approached filling in for it. So, I said a quick prayer—as I always did before a stunt. *Lord keep me safe and protect the crew, the audience, and provide a great performance.* And just like that, any lingering apprehension, guilt, or insecurity I had just disappeared. I then gave a quick look down and calculated my drop. When you do a high fall, the most important thing is to locate your "spot." This was the landing target of your head, and you had to nail it so that your body would be in the correct position when you hit it. Eerily, my "spot" just happened to be the big bloodstain where the previous stuntman had misjudged.

Without any further ado and with every eye on the team watching me, I jumped.

Everything with a major stunt fall comes down to placement, consistency, and practice. With my right foot on the front edge, I pick my spot on the pad where I want my head to land. As I start to fall forward, my right arm goes up as my left leg flexes. This not only provides balance but makes it look like you're flailing to your death, creating a cool effect for the crowd. As I fall headfirst, arms and legs flailing opposite of each other, I never take my eye off my spot. I feel the hot air rush past my face until the crucial moment when I tuck my head into my body, which whips me around so my back is down. If all goes right, I'll land flat on my back with my head laying exactly as planned on my spot. What's not to love? High falls were a passion of mine, and I was known for consistency and accuracy. When I fell, I always hit my spot. I was an asset! The most dangerous part of the high fall, or any stunt for that matter, is complacency. When you get complacent you skimp on the proper placement, fail to maintain consistency, or cease to practice. With thousands of high falls under my belt, I was very confident but never complacent. As confidence builds, fear subsides. And what replaces that? Adrenaline and pride.

It's not a spoiler alert to say that the high fall went without a hitch. And from that point, my time at Six Flags Marine World took off. In just a matter of months after that fall, I became the featured performer on the team, doing more roles, falls, crashes than anyone else in the cast. The park would also expand its shows, adding a Batman water stunt show to the mix. Before I knew it, I was wearing a variety of hats in both shows. I was the most valuable performer at the park. I got to play an Indiana Jones type character, Batman, Bruce Wayne, the Riddler, and just about everybody else from their cast of characters. I did stunt driving of the Batboat, Jet Skis, and zip lines over the audience. On some days I would have to perform in the Indiana Jones–themed Jungle show and then, literally, run to the Batman show to play Batman and back again. And I did this for nearly two years. Life was great at the time. I was at the peak of my physical condition. And I was in a great place both mentally and spiritually. I even managed to make a friend or two. But just as I was settling into my routine as an amusement park stuntman, I was hit with a curveball. And it came with a phone call.

"Hello," I answered.

"Dan, it's Kinnie Gibson."

I was momentarily speechless. It had been two years since I'd met with Kinnie, and we'd barely spoken since.

"Dan, are you there?"

"Oh, hey, Kinnie!" I said, collecting myself. "How are you?"

"I'm good," he said. "Listen, we're going to be on the West Coast, doing a Rocketman show in San Francisco. How'd you like to come down and join the crew?" *Hmm, let me think about . . .* "YES!" I imagined that the next phase of my career and life was about to begin.

I arrived at the 49ers stadium a nervous wreck. I had been around stunt crews for much of my adult life and I knew that most of them are a tightly knit, even tribal, bunch. Sure, there are internal rivalries and petty feuds among them, but they would never let those be visible to an outsider. I also had to imagine that my presence there was surely threatening to a degree. After all, I was, potentially, going to encroach on someone's job, wasn't I? *Is that why I'm here?* I was feeling a bit insecure. There was a big difference between the world I was coming from and the world that Kinnie and his team occupied. I wore a cheap, rubber Batsuit while I fought villains and drove Batboats at a theme park. Kinnie and his Rocketman crew were highly seasoned professionals who traveled the world working with state-of-the-art technology, performing on some of the biggest stages the world had to offer. I assumed that any team involved in that caliber of work would most likely be a bunch of arrogant egomaniacs. However, nothing could have been further from reality.

Kinnie's crew was professional, no doubt. It was filled with some of the smartest people I had ever met. But they were also some of the most humble, kind, and gracious people I've ever been around. As a matter of coincidence, a friend of mine named Sid Goodloe was part of the team. He was the road manager and someone Dave Kilde had introduced me to a few years back, so it was nice to know a familiar face. I met their pilot, Eric Scott, too. Eric was my newest idol at the time. I thought he was one of the best Rocketbelt pilots in the world. And I still do. And he could not have been more welcoming and gracious.

When it came time for the actual show, I didn't really know what to expect. Of course, I had seen television shows and movies that featured someone flying around with a jet pack. Obviously, Boba Fett came to mind for me. I saw James Bond fly one as well in *Thunderball*. Heck, even Michael Jackson flew it out of the stadium during his *Dangerous* tour. (I actually now own that Rocketbelt, too.) So, obviously I had some idea of what to expect. I think pretty much everyone does. Pilot straps on contraption. Pilot turns the throttle. Pilot launches toward the sky. Pilot lands safely. Well, if it were that mundane, *nobody would care*.

There are certain things in life that just cannot be captured or replicated. You can Google the ceiling of the Sistine Chapel and see a photo of Michelangelo's *Creation of Adam*, but in no way does it capture the breadth, depth, and splendor of that masterpiece in person. You can see a video of the Grand Canyon shot in super-high-definition 70-millimeter film from a balloon that hovers above it, but it can never come even close to standing at the foot of that wonder and seeing it for yourself. I know these are lofty comparisons. But there is a reason that during a Rocketman performance, tens of thousands of people watch with bated breath as the pilot hits the throttle. The noise is absolutely deafening. And you can, literally, feel the power of the rocket as it lets out its exhaust in an explosion of raw, unabated thrust. It takes a scientific marvel to break God's law of gravity. And when this law is broken, there is something in our collective consciousness that causes us to do nothing but stop, watch, and admire the feat. And such was the case when I saw it for the first time. There was nothing to do but watch in awe.

I think for the remainder of my time with Kinnie's crew, I just wandered around aimlessly. Eric Scott may have been the one who piloted the Rocketbelt, but I was the one who was still floating on air. It was like I just stayed there, in the moment. It was a dream I didn't want to wake up from. Don't get me wrong, I had carved out a nice life for myself at Marine World, but being a part of a Rocketman show was a tough act to follow. I was quietly praying that there was a reason Kinnie had invited me to San Francisco beyond "meeting the crew."

And my prayer was answered when he called me later and asked if I'd like to go to Texas to "give the belt a try." As he talked to me, I think the first part of his process was just to square me up, to see if I had been spooked by the belt, or if maybe after having seen it fly remained uncertain. But I was unwavering. "I'd love to do that, Kinnie," I told him.

I had never been so sure of anything in all my life.

---

Returning home, I took care of what I needed, asking for some time off from Six Flags, then made arrangements for the trip to Texas. I wasn't sure how long I was going to be there, so I got an open ticket. If things went poorly, I could have wound up returning the same day. *But if they went well?* Maybe I was going to be looking to move.

Kinnie Gibson and his team worked out of a hangar in McKinney, just outside of Dallas. At this time, McKinney was still a small town, not the thriving city it is today. The hangar was at a small, privately run airport that belonged to a small community/neighborhood of aviation enthusiasts. In fact, each house had its own hangar to fly out of. Kinnie's hangar had an apartment upstairs and an office downstairs. The fuel room itself looked like a meth lab or something. There were beakers, pumps, hydrometers, and thirty-gallon drums all over the place. It was a manufacturing plant for hydrogen peroxide, our propellant. To ensure the safety of the performance flights, we made our own in-house to exact specifications, such as percentage and the amount of stabilizers mixed in.

There wasn't much ado about my arrival. It was, if anything, casual. I was shown around the place, met a few other folks on the team who hadn't been in San Francisco, and was given a very quick crash course on how to operate the Rocketbelt. I think this was done purposefully to see how I might handle myself when things went sideways. And have no doubt, when you strap on the Rocketbelt for the first time, things can go sideways in a split second. According to Eric, it was the ability to remain calm that was the pilot's greatest asset. Because achieving liftoff for a human is one of the most unnatural feelings there is. The body and mind will instinctually fight it. And if you fight with the Rocketbelt, you will lose, as I would discover very painfully in due time.

The first time the Rocketbelt was strapped to me, I was struck by how heavy it was. The belt was a somewhat manageable ninety pounds when empty, but fully fueled, it weighed 160 pounds, which was basically just a few pounds less than I weighed. I guess I shouldn't have been surprised at this given its purpose, but it's such a beautiful piece of machinery I was expecting something light and comfortable. The Rocketbelt is neither. It's heavy and unwieldy. And it was also strapped to me as tight as bark on a tree, practically choking the circulation in my legs and shoulders. I wasn't sure if they were doing this on purpose too, maybe making it as unmanageable as they could to see if I would complain. Still, I kept my mouth shut. They could've used a staple gun to attach the thing and I wouldn't have said a word. I wanted to fly. But one of the first things I learned about the Rocketbelt was that *nobody* goes up during training. All flights are "tethered" meaning not only would I be strapped to the Rocketbelt, I would also be strapped to a safety line so I that didn't kill myself.

Once I was finally set, I was given the green light to turn the throttle.

And so I did.

At the outset of a Rocketman launch, it's the sound that is most unsettling. It's something straight out of a horror movie: an ear-splitting chorus of a high-pitched shrieking that matches the tone of my current tinnitus. It was a sound that easily penetrated through my helmet and earplugs—and still I was overwhelmed by it.

I turned the throttle further. Though I was told repeatedly how delicate the throttle was, this is something I could only learn through experience. It was more sensitive than a hair trigger. It was like a follicle trigger. To make things more difficult, it was reverse of a motorcycle throttle, meaning up was down and down was up,

I had barely turned the throttle when I felt a massive surge of rocket combustion envelope me. First it pushed me backward a bit, which I resisted by pushing the control arms down to somewhat of a center point. My feet were still on the ground, but I could feel the Rocketbelt wanting to fly, so I turned into the throttle a little further and gave it more power. I felt my feet leave the ground and lift into the air. My concentration jumped from what I was doing with the handles to the sensation of flight. That's where it all went haywire.

One of the many things that I was warned about before the test was something called "spatial disorientation." Spatial disorientation is that "fight" I mentioned. Gravity is a law of nature. Break it and your mind and body want to know how and why. And that's what mine were wondering the moment I achieved liftoff. Before I could even process it, I was flying sideways. I brought my attention from my feet back to the control arms, but before I could try to correct, the cable caught me and I was fully out of control. I shut off the Rocketbelt and Kinnie gently lowered me back to the ground.

I wish I could say I was a natural. I wish I could say I was in control. But I was neither. The first tethered flight of Daniel Schlund lasted less than eight seconds. And during those last four seconds, I didn't feel like I was flying—I felt more like a bottle rocket on the end of a shoestring. I most certainly would have crashed had it not been for the tether. But Kinnie wasn't looking at my skills yet. He was looking at my mental acuity and my reaction to pressure, which is why as soon as I got settled from my first tethered run I said, "Let's do it again. I know I can do better."

I needed to express to Kinnie that I was not intimidated by the Rocketbelt. I wanted him to know that I was willing to take anything and everything it could give. After all, I was riding motorcycles when I was four and learned to ride a unicycle when I was eight. I learned to stunt drive cars, boats, Jet Skis, and all matters of stunt apparatuses. I knew I could do it with enough training and practice. The unknown factor was how much practice it would take.

Unfortunately, my second tethered flight was only slightly better than the first. I did achieve liftoff and even managed to hover for just a moment, but as I attempted to move forward, I went sideways again, spun out of control, and Kinnie had to lower me back to the ground. Advantage: Rocketbelt.

I returned to California feeling like a bit of a failure. I felt like I had been given my shot at the Holy Grail and I didn't rise to the occasion. Kinnie didn't give me much to go on, simply saying, "Well, we are still considering and will let you know." Even though he said he wasn't looking at my actual flight skills yet, it was impossible to feel good about my inability to handle the Rocketbelt. I know now in retrospect I was set up to fail. The best pilots from the U.S. Air Force would struggle on a Rocketbelt the first time, so why wouldn't a stuntman? Still, my brief brush with the Rocketman team left me depressed and had sapped away much of my self-esteem.

Returning to my job in Vallejo didn't help. While I certainly had the support and love from my family and close friends, many others seemed to take joy in my failure. It was as if my failure had only reinforced their lot in life. Like, "Why try anything bold? Dan did, and look what happened to him."

Despite my sob story, I decided I was not going to wallow in a pity party. I still had a pretty good life and was still living my version of a dream. I also had plenty of work and all kinds of stunt opportunities. But the truth was, the stunt business was not the type of career you retire from after years of service and get a gold watch. It's a young person's game, and as you get older, nobody's body can hold it together. I had been doing it as a springboard to larger things and had no real plan if the work never came to fruition. But just as I reconciled the fact that my dream job wasn't going to come through, Kinnie called again. And he had very encouraging news. Kind of.

"Dan," he said. "We'd like you to come to McKinney. I've got a job for you."

"What kind of job?" I wondered.

"Well," he said. "We're gonna train you to fly, Dan, but what I also need is someone who will work. I need someone to handle the propellant and some of the other aspects of the business. You've done events and the team likes you. I think you'd be perfect."

I thought about Kinnie's proposition. Obviously, I would've given my right leg (pun intended) to be one of his pilots, but I wasn't prepared to leave my life behind and uproot to Texas to manufacture fuel and help organize his events. So, I asked him what I really needed to know.

"Do you think there's a chance I could be a pilot eventually?"

"I'm not going promise you anything, Dan," he said. "A lot of people tried in the past with no luck. But if you work hard and I think you're ready, we'll see what happens."

It was good enough for me. All I needed was to get my foot in the door.

# 7

# Rocket Helper

In October of 2000, I left my stunt job at Six Flags Marine World a few weeks early and moved to McKinney, Texas, to work full-time for Kinnie Gibson and his Rocketman company, Powerhouse Productions. I didn't arrive in McKinney with any delusions. I figured, at the very least, that in my time with Kinnie and his team I would learn a great deal, travel to new places with the team, and then return home having been on a few adventures. But I would be lying if I said I didn't want and expect more. I left my stunt job early expecting to start training immediately, but it wouldn't be for another month or so. I felt bad for abandoning my team (which they were certainly not happy about) when a few weeks wouldn't have mattered in the long run. But I knew deep inside I would be a terrific pilot, so my biggest challenge was to just simply be an asset, work hard, and temper my enthusiasm to be trained.

My job with Kinnie began as an apprenticeship, and as such I was not paid during my training. Team members generally didn't get paid until a performance was booked. I didn't think this would be a problem as I thought we'd be doing shows almost immediately, but that wasn't the case. It would be months before my first show, and things had gotten pretty dicey for me. I had rented a small, one-bedroom apartment in Dallas, but with no income and bills, I burnt through what little money I had saved like, well, like rocket fuel. In fact, it got so bad that after a few months Kinnie let me move into a small apartment in the hangar at a very reasonable rate.

The first order of my responsibilities was learning how to procure, distill, and store the propellant (the fuel) for the Rocketbelt. The propellant was the very lifeblood of the entire Rocketman enterprise. It was hard to get. Harder to make. And highly dangerous. It was incredibly corrosive, and it needed to be stowed carefully in specialized Teflon-lined drums. Interestingly, what most people don't know, and I certainly didn't, is that the propellant isn't combustible. It's actually just hydrogen peroxide. But not the heavily diluted hydrogen peroxide you find in your medicine cabinet, which is actually only 3 percent by volume. The propellant we used is close to 90 percent pure hydrogen peroxide, making it highly corrosive to any kind of organic material such as plants, cotton, leather, and, of course, boots—as I would later find out.

Between my fuel work and the odd jobs around the hangar, a few months flew by as I fell into the rhythm of the place. We had started flight training but it was a very slow process.

Toward the beginning, Kinnie drove me to lunch and we had a very personal, potent conversation during which he evoked the timeless theatrical notion of *the show must go on*. I remember him explaining: "This is a long-term investment. You in me and me in you. It is likely that we will disagree and even argue in the future. Despite our relationship, the Rocketman image, our dedication to professionalism, they must rise beyond any issues we might have."

Not only did I understand what Kinnie was saying, I wholeheartedly agreed. It was a speech similar to those I'd made with stuntmen and stuntwomen under my productions. Although Kinnie and I would have our disagreements indeed, I never took it out on a performance or the Rocketman brand.

So, I worked hard, trained harder, and eventually my responsibilities expanded into the rest of the business. I then started helping Sheri run the day-to-day operations, and together we handled all aspects of the company. The business side of things appealed to me; since I had experience running my own crews, especially in Taiwan, I was actually quite adept at managing and organizing events on a global scale. Handling things like shipping, visas, plane tickets, and negotiations for our performances were all second nature to me.

Meanwhile, Sheri handled the more complex aspects of the business, such as the money and the contracts.

Besides building and maintaining the Rocketbelts and propellant, Kinnie would often travel with us when he wasn't working on *Walker, Texas Ranger* to make sure all the details of the performance, including me, ran safely and smoothly.

Fuel, as I mentioned, was always an issue. If I thought it was hard to make, traveling with it was even more difficult. Every destination carried different site procedures, protocols, and politics. As for the Rocketbelt itself, that was a whole other issue. Some places didn't even know how to categorize it technologically. Was it a piece of equipment? Was it an aircraft? Was it "stunt equipment"? Thankfully, Sheri knew how to cut through all the red tape and knew a lot of shortcuts—and for those she didn't know, she knew how to get to the person who did. And she taught me just about everything.

Soon enough, I was promoted to Director of Operations. So, in addition to the thrill of learning to fly the Rocketbelt, I carried a fancy title and assisted Sheri, who continued handling the money and contracts while I handled the logistics of each performance, including client negotiations, plane tickets, visas, shipment of the propellant, the Rocketbelt, technical riders, and all the other equipment that went with it. But once the contract was signed, my job was just beginning. During shows I acted as manager for the team, dealing with the client as well as on-site issues and coordinating the performance itself. It was a crash course in global logistics and culture. On a few occasions I had to deal with corrupt government officials, mafia bosses, and even the KGB—sometimes all of the above. Luckily for me, the clients who hired us usually outranked all that would stand in our way and somehow managed to push things through if we ever hit a wall. I was never forced or asked to pay a bribe, but I can't say the same about the clients—then again, I never asked.

I was learning nearly every aspect of the Rocketman enterprise: maintenance, logistics, chemistry, physics, legal, and now piloting. Kinnie strategically kept some of the secret details to himself as an insurance policy since others in the past had tried to exploit him from time to time. In one instance, before I came on board, a Rocketbelt technician—not to mention a friend of Kinnie's—stole the blueprints and built his own Rocketbelt. The story of the RB2000 is a cautionary tale of greed and deception leading to deterioration of the group—then to the murder of one member, the kidnapping of another person, and prison sentences for those involved. While normally this is the kind of drama that's depicted in movies, this event in Rocketbelt history is highlighted in my documentary. Through the years, the Rocketman organization worked very hard to remove ourselves from that drama.

Besides the tremendous amount of work that went into planning and performing a show, the experience exceeded all of my greatest expectations of adventure. With each arrival in a foreign country, we were treated as foreign dignitaries by officials and as celebrities by the public. And every place we stopped we were given the red-carpet treatment. This included police escorts, comped meals at the hosts' best restaurants, box seats for any event we wanted to attend while there, and VIP invitations for the biggest parties you could imagine. As a young and single man, I indulged in many of the perks that were thrown my way, but now that I reflect on it, I have some remorse. While I wasn't totally out of control, I didn't always live by the standard that was given to me by my parents. I made some mistakes and wrote them off as being "young and single." And I was only the Director of Operations at the time. Things would become far more challenging for me when I actually became a pilot.

Despite any indiscretions I may have had while abroad, I did take as much time as I could to absorb as much culture as possible while visiting another country—especially places I quite literally didn't even know existed. Turkmenistan ended up being one of my favorite places. The architecture was beautiful, and the people were friendly. But it was also an oppressive dictatorship. They didn't use credit cards; everything was in cash, their currency being the manat. One manat was worth $0.29, and the highest denomination at the time was 100 manats, but you wouldn't get a fair shake at the bank, so our driver would bring us to the underbelly of Turkmenistan to trade our hundred-dollar bills for a big stack of manats. It felt like we were doing a drug deal. At the restaurants, when it came time to pay, instead of a flat envelope to slip your cash into, they would bring a small box and use money counters to tally up the bill.

We also did a few flights in Venezuela before and after it was turned into a dictatorship. Before, there was plenty of nightlife, lots of shops to visit, and an overall feeling of being in Florida. After, it seemed like it was devoid of life, most of the shops shut down and the nightlife only a pale vestige of former days. The people didn't have any money. We did one flight for a "No Vote" event, a demonstration against the additional term of the dictator at the time. There were hundreds of thousands of people, and once our pilot, Eric, landed, we had to shuttle him to a nearby van to escape any potential repercussions—something I didn't know till we were on site. Later that night, Jimmy Carter came to validate the vote. (Guess who won?) We hadn't been back to Venezuela since.

We went to Holland, and I got to see some of my old stunt friends. Being familiar with the language and culture, it was nice to be back in town, though our performance there was one of one of our less remarkable ones—for a truck competition. From there we moved on to Nicaragua, where the flight, although a success, was only seventeen seconds long. Atypical to the normal average of twenty-six seconds. A short flight for Eric was unusual, and the client asked for another performance. I reminded them of the agreed-upon cost for the second flight and they were not happy. One of my Rocketbelt technicians and a successful stuntman, J.J. Perry, was with us at the time. He spoke the language, and after overhearing the conversation the clients were having, led me away, explaining, "I think we should go." The client was not happy with the price. Eric stated he would fly, but it was up to me. Being a company man, I stuck to the price, and we didn't fly again. In hindsight, just accepting what they were offering to pay for the second flight would have been the right thing to do. Happy clients lead to more flights, period. We left Nicaragua in good order, but I learned that I should have exercised my managerial authority and been more flexible, instead of being too worried over what Kinnie would have thought if I changed the agreement on-site.

Of course, one of my final responsibilities on each gig as Director of Operations was getting everything and everyone back to Texas in one piece. And believe it or not, sometimes this was the hardest aspect of my job. We take for granted now how easy it is to run a business in America. Things like taxis, plane tickets, and shipping are all a phone call or a click away. Not so much overseas, especially before smartphones became the rage. If our travel plans ever changed in the least bit, it could take all day to sort out. And God forbid any one of us misplaced a passport or got into some kind of trouble. As a general rule, we tried to stick together. But we were also all adults with varied tastes and had different ideas of what "leisure time" meant. Some of us liked to see the sights, some liked to dabble in the local cuisine, and others preferred to spend their time back at our hotel. But some were more "free-spirited."

To be blunt, Eric was a pain in the ass to manage. I loved the guy. Still do. But he was so effusively confident with his rock star mentality that it was hard to manage him. I was the new guy, or as he called me, the "Golden Boy," so he pretty much did what he wanted when we were off the clock. One time when we were in Japan, we had to get to the airport to fly to Jakarta, Indonesia, for another performance. Our flight was early the next day, so I made it a point for the team to be in our rooms at a certain time. Needless to say, Eric didn't do well with curfews, I simply went to bed, but I suspect Eric went out. Being a pilot myself now, I get it, you need to blow off some steam—a lot of steam!—before and after a flight. Early the next day, though, the client by my side, I went to Eric's room and knocked on the door—no answer. I called security to open the door but he had left the chain on it, so they couldn't open it all the way. However, it was opened just enough for me to see him on the bed, snoring away like a busted chainsaw.

"Eric! Wake up, man! We've got TO GO!" I yelled.

But he just kept sleeping. He was always a heavy sleeper. I thought about kicking the door and breaking the chain, but you have to be very careful with committing any kind of crime in a foreign country, especially with a security guard next to you, so I had no choice but to simply let him sleep. I had to get to the airport to ship the equipment, which was going to be a whole other sensitive negotiation in itself. So, I left him there, informed the front desk, and left him some money to find his own way to Indonesia. Needless to say, when he eventually arrived the next day, he was pretty angry. "We don't leave our men behind!" he lectured me.

I told him that this wasn't exactly *Platoon* and that I had tried, but he needed to be more responsible. To this day he still ribs me about it.

One of the things you quickly learn about doing shows abroad is that sometimes you can plan an event to the T, taking into consideration every plausible or implausible contingency you can imagine, and something will still go wrong.

Things like shipping deadlines, missed ships, planes, and visa procedures were usually the most closely watched part of my job. It's the unforeseeable that throws a wrench into the plan. And the unforeseeable can be both costly and, in some situations, dangerous.

Such was the case for the show we had booked in Saudi Arabia. Arab and Asian countries are particularly sensitive to deal with. Not only is there a huge cultural difference that makes communication and common understanding challenging, but when it comes to business they are absolutely by the book. Everything had to be done according to the signed contract. Sheri and I had done our homework and planned the show to perfection. The entire team arrived on time and without any hassles. The Rocketbelt came by air freight, but the propellant could not travel on airplanes, so it was always shipped by ocean liner and later delivered to us at the show location. When it finally came time to check our equipment, everything was there except the most important thing—the fuel! The shipper missed a connection and the fuel was not going to make it in time. And there was nothing I or anyone else could do about it.

Rocketbelt fuel wasn't something we could just whip up or buy locally, even in a rich country like Saudi Arabia full of fuel resources. Our propellant, like the Rocketbelt itself, is very exacting. Our hydrogen peroxide is extremely pure; the wrong concentration of stabilizers could cause disaster—as when Kinnie almost lost his foot in a crash due to bad peroxide. In short, basically no one used it, and if they did, I wasn't going to risk my life or the life of the pilot on it. It all had to be right or it was a no-go. So, we told the client that we couldn't do the performance.

If only it were that easy. Saudis have incredible pride, and nobody on the client's side wanted to take responsibility for the delayed fuel. Since we booked the shipment, we were most culpable, even though the mistake was not ours. Well, that put the onus on Kinnie and our team. If we accepted fault, we could've been in breach of contract. Not only would that be incredibly costly, but if found guilty, we might've gone to jail. Who knows? We then had to find a solution that would allow our team to exit the country without incident while the client could also "save face." It was then agreed that Eric and I would do an appearance with the Rocketbelt, but we wouldn't fly it. It would be more like a show-and-tell for this client's very high-end festival. Kinnie made them sign an agreement that would ensure our departure and that guaranteed we wouldn't stand trial for breach of contract. After all was said and done, the whole affair ended up being one of the more interesting "performances" I had ever been a part of. Eric and I ended up going to what was a very nice and expensive vacation. We shook hands and shared stories, showing off the Rocketbelt in a very public setting. That was until the Saudi religious police unexpectedly showed up with thin sticks in hand, tapping the Quran, and separated all the men from the women and children. The women and children are supposed to be separated from men in public. Even the Wendy's I went to had separate sections for men and families, which basically meant the women and children were separated from the men at all times. I didn't get involved, but I conversed with everyone the same despite the looks of hatred I got from the religious police.

Although we didn't get to do a real show, I came away from the experience very intrigued by Saudi Arabia. It was an incredibly quiet country and perhaps one of the most isolated and peculiar places I had ever seen. There were lots of beggars. Women's faces on the covers and pages of magazines were blocked out with a sharpie. There were countless neon green towers everywhere, representing the various mosques. I went to order a pizza for delivery and a recording instructed me to "call again after prayer time." Five times a day, the loudspeakers shouted out prayers. I was also struck by how the women carried themselves; I was expecting them to be timid and deferential, but what stood out to me most was how confident and incredibly educated they were. They were curious, articulate, and, most of all, welcoming. They appeared incredibly refined and spoke nearly perfect English, though I felt a distance from them as they were covered head to toe. In private places, though, they were allowed to take off their burkas and dress fashionably.

On my way back to the airport, I was feeling a bit melancholic about the whole trip. I had grown accustomed to the pure blast of adrenaline a show delivered, but my trip to Saudi Arabia had provided something different: the opportunity to really stop and reflect on what the world is really like for the vast majority of people. By now I had worked in over a dozen countries. And while some of them were absolutely beautiful places where I'd meet some wonderful people, every country we performed in came with warnings. We were warned what to say, what not to say. What to do. Where to go. Where not to go. Nobody is ever given any such warning when coming to the United States.

Yes, there are some rough areas in some of the bigger cities—I know having worked in them during my ambulance days. But in our country, you can say what you want. You can do what you want. And you can go where you want, when you want. I was reminded of the difference when I was being driven along the road from Damascus to the airport in Riyadh, Christmas Day, 2000. It was a lonely, open stretch of road with wild camels strewn throughout the desert around it. The driver had to stop at a little dusty and desolate oasis that made for a gas station. I stepped out, bought a Coke in a faded glass bottle and made a final call to the airlines to assure my travel and the shipment of the Rocketbelt. After the call, I sifted through some of the apps on my phone. One of them was an app for the Bible. Bibles were illegal in Saudi Arabia, so I'd left mine at home. It later occurred to me, had officials gone through my phone, I might have been arrested and, possibly, would still be in a Saudi prison to this day.

# 8

# Blood, Sweat, and Fears

While I enjoyed working in Operations for Team Rocketman, it was not what I had uprooted myself from California to do. I had moved in the hope that I would eventually become a pilot. But after a year, it seemed a dream that always remained at arm's length.

There were several factors that played into the delay. One was the simple cost of the training. Making propellent was a time-consuming and costly endeavor with one full tank costing over a thousand dollars and twenty-four hours to make. And not only was it expensive, it didn't last long. Each full tank was only good for thirty seconds. And for training purposes, the flight time was broken into three ten-second intervals, which we called "hops." It made what was already "intermittent training" all the more difficult. Imagine learning to drive a car only ten seconds at a time.

Another factor that most assuredly made Kinnie reluctant was the cold fact that I just wasn't very good. Though I had the courage and temperament to handle the Rocketbelt, I had never been a gifted athlete and struggled with the physical aspect of piloting the Rocketbelt. Even in my prior stunt work, it took longer than average to learn my choreography. Piloting the Rocketbelt was another level entirely. It takes a great deal of balance and coordination to navigate taking off, advancing, and turning and landing, and I had a hard time with almost all of the above. As I mentioned earlier, in the other stunts success was down to placement, consistency, and practice. The difference with piloting the Rocketbelt is that placement is more sensitive; there's less room for error with more deadly risk. I'd even flown an airplane a number of times, but the controls between a plane and Rocketbelt are night and day. A quick movement you might make in an airplane yoke would throw the Rocketbelt spinning out of control. (The secret is to be sure your thrust tubes are pointed straight down the best you can.) Then the instant you go full throttle you need to find your "center" or "placement" before you can start to maneuver. This all happens in a blink of an eye. And with training flights only sporadic and at ten-second intervals, improvement came at a snail's pace. But I knew myself. It would take me some time to get it, but once I got something, it was locked in for life.

Despite my personal struggles with the Rocketbelt, my job with Kinnie was going splendidly. So good, in fact, that I was promoted once again to Managing Director for the company. This came with even more responsibility and latitude to make decisions, including handling complex contracts and negotiations. The good news was that my career was advancing. The Rocketman enterprise was doing great business, and by now I was very much a part of their success. The bad news was: It wasn't as a pilot yet.

---

While business was going great for the Rocketman team, our type of business was anything but consistent. Our performances catered to a very specific audience. We had "runs" in different parts of the world. For a while Australia and New Zealand was hot, then South America, then the Asian countries. We provided "event" entertainment that was justifiably expensive, usually in the tens of thousands of dollars. It wasn't like we were doing ribbon cuttings at your local supermarket. To that end, it's not like our phone was ringing off the hook. Most of our performances were planned months or even years in advance. And because travel was such a grind, it took considerable logistical work to book more than two shows per month. Yes, there were times we did more, sometimes back-to-back events, like flying on a Learjet to get from the Indy 500 to Trinidad and Tobago and back in twenty-four hours. Sometimes we'd do the same show at the same venue for several nights in a row. But there were also times we did less, and there were dry periods where we did no performances at all. During those periods, to keep myself busy, I'd get back into doing stunt work. Thanks to Kinnie's relationship with Chuck Norris, I would do occasional stunts for *Walker, Texas Ranger*, but since the series was coming to an end, I didn't get as much as I'd hoped for. I did work on a whole slew of movie sets, including *Vampires Suck*, *The Good Guys*, and *Walking Tall Part 2*. I even doubled Channing Tatum on *Stop-Loss*. But the film and television industry just didn't want me. For me, it was too much of a "who you know" business. Meanwhile, while I enjoyed performing for a camera, I liked performing in front of people a lot more. I loved the joy they received and the energy they gave me. I had always known live action was the road God had laid out for me—and I was also convinced that it would be the Rocketbelt I'd use to take me there.

It was at this time that I began to push for more training. I didn't care how expensive it was or how long it took, I was going to turn myself into a great pilot. But as my sporadic training continued, it became very clear that I still wasn't doing so hot. Kinnie was hoping to make a movie and was needing more than one pilot to make the movie, and at the same time we wanted to do more live performances. All in all, backups were needed if anything happened to one pilot or another.

At its most basic, the typical flight with the Rocketbelt is one of liftoff, ascension, flying to a designated target, and landing safely. That's pretty simple. It wasn't as if I was going to be asked to fly an obstacle course or navigate through a dense and dark terrain (though that happened from time to time). But it still needed to be done to perfection. A pilot could not veer off with even the slightest deviation. At most of our events, our very simple course was designed in the midst of tens of thousands of people. Think of a parade or a sporting event. If you're flying above or near a crowd of people and you veer off course and something happens, the result could be a mass-casualty event. In this case it would be like throwing a refrigerator into the stands from fifty feet. In other words, there was a reason for our meticulous training. A flight *had to be perfect*. It was just too dangerous not to be.

While the crowd and our audience were always our greatest concern, there's another reason a flight needed to be perfect: the pilot themself, for whom there was always the possibility of ending up severely injured or even killed. At the time, this was something I still had not fully comprehended, truly did not understand the danger of what I wanted to do. I can't say that it was hubris; I knew that there was risk involved. But my problem was that I looked at flying the Rocketbelt as no different than any other elaborate stunts I had learned to do over the years. My success merely depended on a simple equation: If I did A, B, and C correctly, I would be able to pull anything off. Unfortunately for me, success with the Rocketbelt came with no such equation—and this was a lesson that would take me years to discover. Until then, I needed to learn the basics. I had to fly more on instinct than calculations, much like driving a stick-shift.

In the beginning, I started out at a lower pressure of thrust so as to get the feeling of balancing the Rocketbelt. This alone takes an enormous amount of practice. It's one thing to feel "free flight," but it's another to have that same feeling while being strapped to a 160-pound piece of equipment. And only when my balance was mastered would the belt be allowed to go full pressure so that movement and flight could be achieved. Remember that each training flight consisted of three "hops," those ten-second intervals. Well, as the Rocketbelt got lighter after each hop, it took a moment to adjust because each launch would happen with more force than the previous. In other words, the throttle would become more sensitive as fuel weight was expended. I was also still finding it incredibly tough to absorb that the throttle, in addition to being hypersensitive, worked opposite how they always had in my experience. I had grown up on motorcycles and learned at a very young age that you give the bike gas by dropping the throttle with your wrist. This is a universal movement that everybody who's ever ridden a motorcycle or even a dirt bike understands. The same thing holds true for giving your car gas while driving. You "hit the gas" going down on the pedal. Well, with the Rocketbelt it's the opposite. The throttle goes *up*. Imagine driving a car where you pull on the gas pedal instead of pushing on it.

Whenever I trained, we would go through two to three tanks a day, or about nine hops. The goal was to give me a mastery of lifting off smoothly, moving forward in a straight line, and finishing with a controlled landing.

When I absolutely mastered those three phases of flight, I would be ready to get off the cable. Now, you would think that after a year of "tethered flying" and well over $100,000 in propellent costs I would have at least been competent at performing these very basic and fundamental skills. But much to my disappointment (and Kinnie's), I still could not fly in a straight line. No matter how hard I tried, as soon as I took off, I would begin to veer right, and whenever I tried to overcompensate for this, I would spin out of control. It wasn't merely frustrating. It was maddening.

But one day something happened that would change everything for me. It was actually a day that Eric was practicing. And in all honesty, Eric didn't need much practicing.

Eric may have been a wild child who was hard to manage and didn't think much of rules or curfews, but man, that guy could fly a Rocketbelt. Though only slightly shorter than me, he was one hundred fifty pounds of whipcord muscle. And not only was he fearless, he was downright arrogant when it came to being a Rocketbelt pilot. Every time he strapped it on, he would make it clear that *he* controlled the belt, not the other way around. Well, we had to send the training belt to a show, and Eric came by to do a test hop on it before we packed it up, so he used mine.

But as he took off and started flying, I noticed something: He too was drifting off to the right. It only lasted a moment, because being the pilot Eric was, he managed to corral the belt at his whim and continued his practice flight without incident. But I took note. And when he came down, I asked him about it. As an inexperienced pilot, I had thought there was something wrong with me, but as he verified, there was actually something off with the Rocketbelt. The techs took a look and as it turned out, the left thrust tube happened to be slightly longer than the right, causing the flight path to veer off course. They quickly made the fix and I was prepped to go back up. It turned out that all throughout my training to that point, my constant veering right and my lack of control was the fault of that elongated left tube. For an experienced pilot like Eric, he could find his center much easier, but for a new pilot like me, it was like flying an airplane with one wing longer than the other.

It gave me a new shot of confidence to know that the struggles I'd been beating myself up about were actually an equipment problem, and I was initially eager to try my newly recalibrated belt. But then, for the first time in my Rocketbelt training, I found myself feeling nervous. Now, any mistakes on the flight would be mine and mine alone. On one hand, it was a great weight lifted off of me. But on the other hand, the pressure to perform had replaced it. By now, I had really become an integral part of the Rocketman team who was both liked and well-respected. But I knew there had to be some internal grumbling about my exploits with the Rocketbelt. At this point, a year after I had started, it almost seemed a waste of time, as if Kinnie was just being kind to me for all my hard work. And while the staff had been patient with me, I could tell their frustrations had been growing as well. Had I continued to struggle, Kinnie would have had no choice but to just abandon the idea—and he wouldn't have gotten much resistance. And had that happened, I'm not sure I'd blame him. It was time to put up or shut up.

I strapped on the belt and tethered up. At this point, those two things were the only parts of being a Rocketman I had truly mastered. *At least I look like a Rocketman*, I remember thinking despondently to myself at the time. I then mentally prepared myself and said a quick prayer. Typically, just before a flight I would smile at the crew and say something like, "Okay, here we go again." But for this practice run, I stayed in the moment. There was no smiling or self-deprecating announcement before takeoff. I simply turned the throttle.

At the very moment of thrust it felt different. For the first time I had ever been on the belt, it didn't feel like it was a piece of equipment weighing me down. Instead, it felt like an extension of myself. *It felt natural.* For the first time, I was actually *centered*, controlling the belt. Not the other way around. My earlier flights had always seemed chaotic. The piercing sound of the Rocketbelt blocked out everything and I could only see with tunnel vision, and every practice flight seemed to finish in a flash. It was like entering a vortex in the hopes that I would just come out the other end in one piece. But this time when I took off, everything happened slowly. I saw *everything*. And I could hear too. I hadn't entered a vortex; instead, it was as if I caught the perfect wave that *I* controlled. I had lifted off smoothly, flew directly straight to my mark, and landed like I had done it a thousand times. It was perfect. And as soon as I shut off the throttle, the belt's overwhelming noise faded and was replaced with the applause from my teammates. I immediately wanted to go back up untethered. But I wasn't going to. I still needed a few good flights under my belt before Kinnie would risk his machine (or my life for that matter). I did a few more on the tether to show I had hurdled this challenge. I was done with the tether. My next flight was going to be on my own.

---

There is a fine line you hover over, literally, when flying the Rocketbelt. On one side is the unbridled desire to succeed in a spectacular way, pushing the machine to its limit and really providing a spectacle for anyone who watches. The other is the inherent and natural fear that stifles that desire. The goal of the Rocketman is to fly right between both lines—and then to slowly push the envelope when you feel ready for the next challenge. And that's exactly the frame of mind I took to my first free flight. I wasn't going to push. But I wasn't going to hold back either. I suppose it's the same kind of feeling a high-wire walker experiences when the safety net is removed from underneath them. *I just couldn't think about it.*

One of the core characteristics to succeed in any endeavor is confidence. Heck, Eric had it in spades. In fact, Eric had so much confidence it bordered on arrogance. While I had confidence, it was much lower on the spectrum. I trusted my skill and the work I had put in, but I was still nervous about the unknown. Anything could happen once I was up in the air. And the truth was, despite my recent mastery after the recalibration of my belt, I would have experienced horrible crashes dozens of times over had I not been on the cable. And what if the Rocketbelt handled differently without the tether? I didn't know. And I wouldn't know until I went up.

Though it was unintentional, Kinnie didn't help much when he asked me to sign some legal paperwork before my first free flight. I was told it was absolutely standard protocol and I totally understood, but still, it wasn't exactly a vote of confidence being made to sign a document that basically said, "Hey, if you die or get horribly injured on this flight, it's not our fault." And not only did I have to sign it, I had to do a video release too, staring into the camera and verbally releasing the Rocketbelt company from any liability for anything awful that might happen to me. Of course, I did both without any question. This was nevertheless a little extreme for stunt work. We always signed waivers, but there was workers' compensation insurance to cover injuries. In this case, at least during training, there was no workers comp, and I had to provide my own health insurance. It was just how the field was striped, and I agreed to play by the rules before me. So, I didn't just say the words, I accepted them wholeheartedly.

The truth is, had something happened I would have never sued over something I'd agreed to. I just wasn't raised that way. I liked Kinnie and the team and not only knew what I was getting into, I was pleading for it. But there was an even larger truth in play: I really wasn't concerned about getting hurt. Yes, I was aware of the possibility, but fear never entered the equation for me. I'd done thousands of high falls and had been on fire a thousand times as well, and never once did I get hurt. For me, the real fear was disappointing Kinnie and his team. From the time I had met Sheri and she saw something in me that I didn't even know was there, to my introduction to Kinnie, his family and his team, and on through my training, I was nothing but grateful for everything. My biggest motivation was just to not let them down. So I needed to validate their faith in me.

The preparation for the free flight was no different than a flight on the cable. I suited up in my Nomex heat- and flame-resistant undergear, knee pads, and flight suit. Before we could fly, we'd set the pressure in the propellant tanks using a pressure regulator designed for satellites. Inevitably, I'd need to off-gas some of the main tank's pressure to adjust to the correct psi—and I'd need to do it quickly to keep enough operating pressure in the main air tank. This is always done by the pilot, as it's his craft and his responsibility to set the pressure he wants. The next step is to send a bit of propellant through the catalyst (motor) to warm it up. We do a procedure called "burping" the motor. With a quick turn of the throttle, the catalyst is instantly heated to hundreds of degrees Fahrenheit. This allows for a quick and clean decomposition of the propellant; without it, the tanks would belch out an ugly cloud of white steam and the belt's performance would suffer. Once pressurized, the Rocketbelt is ready to fly.

The strap-in procedure consists of squeezing into what we call the corset, a fiberglass backboard that straps around your body and holds you snuggly to the Rocketbelt. The technicians begin strapping in the various buckles. Legs go first, often followed by a myriad of jokes as a poor tech would be eye level with the pilot's nether region. Next comes the waist strap, followed by the shoulder straps, which are pulled so tightly snug that you can literally feel the compression on your spine. Then earplugs in and helmet on, and I'd be ready for the crew to release the holding pins from the stands. I'd transfer the 160-pound Rocketbelt from the stand onto my legs, and then do some control-placement checks. Then I'm ready to fly.

The course for the free flight would be exactly the same, save for the cables and staff who manned them. The only thing that was different was that this time, Kinnie would be behind me, standing as close as he could. He wore welding gloves—just in case something went wrong and he had to grab the scalding-hot tubes. We went through all the pre-launch checks: double-checking the straps, tightening anything that needed tightening, making sure the yaw handle was centered, and removing the throttle lock. I then straightened and braced for launch, legs together and looking straightforward as I picked my "spot" to land.

Finally, on April 19, 2001, I gathered myself, said my prayer, and without further hesitation I turned the throttle and lifted off very smoothly.

It was a great liftoff, nice and straight. I had wondered if flying without the cable would feel different—and it did. To my surprise and relief, it was actually easier to fly off the cable than on it. There was no tugging or rattling of the cord. It felt like I was being lifted by a crane. It may have been psychological, but I actually felt freer in the air. Uninhibited.

About fifteen feet up, I focused on my landing spot and touched down beautifully. It was a textbook flight.

As soon as I landed, I was deluged with congratulatory hugs and handshakes. And at this point in history, I would be only the eleventh person to have successfully free-flown a Rocketbelt. For context, more people walked on the moon than flew a Rocketbelt off-tether. I was bursting with pride and joy. In fact, I don't know if I had ever been happier. Naturally, the first thing that came out of my mouth after the buzz of my first flight settled was "Let's do it again!"

---

That Kinnie did not let me go back up immediately after my first successful flight was one of the great lessons I had ever received in my life. Even after

I pushed a bit, he calmly said, "Let's leave it on a good note. We'll go back up tomorrow."

Of course, I was disappointed, but I just didn't understand. My ego was telling me, "Let's strike while the iron is hot! I'm feeling good! Let's do it!" And while my exuberance was warranted to a degree, Kinnie was teaching me a very important element of being a professional Rocketbelt pilot. And that was to *never get overconfident.* That doesn't mean giving into fear; it means that a pilot has to fly with a *respect* for fear.

Unfortunately, I didn't give much thought at the time to Kinnie's sage reasoning about sleeping on my success, because the next day I was even more excited to go up. With my nerves completely gone, I knew exactly what to expect. I had no fear of crashing and had already proved to Kinnie and the team that I was worthy. I was also excited for the fact that I had moved even closer to my dream of being a Rocketman. In my mind, the real training was just beginning. Soon, I would be the one going out to events. I would be the one performing for folks. And I would be the one in front of the spotlight, not behind it.

For my second flight, I decided to go just a little bit higher and longer. Nothing ridiculous, just another step forward to my larger goal. As I did the previous day (and hundreds of times before), I performed my preflight checklist, said my prayer, and took off.

Boom. Perfect. More congratulatory hugs and handshakes.

I asked to go back up again. And again, Kinnie passed, scheduling my third solo flight for the following day.

What made this flight so special was that it was on the fortieth anniversary of the first-ever Rocketbelt flight performed by Hal Graham, April 20, 1961.

And to top it off, Hal happened to call me that day. I had never talked to him before and he didn't know I did the flight. I guess he was feeling nostalgic. He and I had a great conversation. He was so inspirational and encouraging. We talked about his adventures and flight experiences, shared fears, and discussed what got him in and out of flying the Rocketbelt. He told me stories about flying for dignitaries, even for JFK, and later a crash that knocked him out once. That is when he said he "decided to retire" and explained to me how he had experienced all that could be experienced. He decided not to tempt fate any longer.

The next day couldn't come fast enough. After all, three successful solo flights would ostensibly put me on the road to becoming a Rocketman. It meant that I was ready to start learning more complex maneuvers such as turns, and striving for even greater heights. The cable flights were just the beginning; the free flights were the next phase. And at this point, it was basically a *fait accompli*. I had cracked the code of the Rocketbelt. I was controlling it. It was, quite literally, like riding a bike for me at that point. To that end, for my third free flight, I decided to go even higher and further than I had the previous day. In the past, I had only tried to fly as high as the safety cable would allow. But for this third free flight, I was going to stretch myself.

I prepped.

I pre-checked.

I prayed.

And I went up.

Lo and behold, my third free flight seemed to be the easiest I had ever attempted. I lifted off the ground with a grace I had never felt before, by far the smoothest I had ever experienced. And as I began to fly, it was as if everything I had ever worked for in my ambition to be a Rocketman had finally and fully coalesced. All the insecurities, fears, and failures were gone. I simply left them behind as I soared to what I believed to be my destiny: my vocation as a Bona Fide Rocketman. Visions of my future glory flashed before me. I could see myself flying over parades and launching off of stages, and I felt the eyes of tens of thousands of people upon me . . .

I found my spot and gently descended toward it, lowering until my toes kissed the ground.

But then something happened. Instead of turning the throttle off immediately, I was a split second late and I bounced back up into the air nearly four feet. I didn't panic. I had trained for this. I was simply going to recenter myself and just land at another spot. However, Kinnie, seeing the potential disaster, grabbed the back of the Rocketbelt to keep me from jetting into the hangar.

What happened next occurred very quickly. I felt myself veer off to the right and I slammed into the ground. I then either blacked out or was concussed. I still don't know exactly what happened, but I don't remember anything after crashing—and that was probably a blessing. Because as I laid on the ground unconscious, the Rocketbelt was still on and it was blasting

1,200-degree steam at Mach 3 right into my right leg and backside. To make matters worse, because I had landed on my right side, both the throttle and the emergency shut-off valve were imbedded in the ground. As a result, Kinnie and members of the team couldn't get to it. They desperately tried to turn me over, the thrust blasting off their hearing protection, but it was nearly three hundred pounds of dead weight—with a rocket motor churning out a stream of scalding-hot steam as the other crew members held my legs to keep me from skipping across the ground. As they frantically tried to kill the throttle, my entire backside and thighs were being incinerated—for a good ten to fifteen seconds, from what I was told—by the super-heated exhaust. I assumed they released the straps once the apparatus was off and rolled me out, but I had lost consciousness. The only thing my team could do from then was wait for the ambulance and deal with the hearing damage.

In the back of the ambulance, the team laid hands on me and prayed. And though I was not able to hear their prayers, I know that God did. It was a blessing that I had blacked out, and to this day, I am still grateful.

My blessing of oblivion, however, was to be short-lived. Because the next time I was coherent enough to think clearly, it would be from a bed in the McKinney Community Hospital emergency room.

# 9

# Crashed

I woke up to the chaos of nurses hovering over me. I was attached to what seemed a half-dozen monitors of various types and all were beeping like mad. My clothes had been cut off and the entire lower half of my body was covered in gauze save for my lower legs and feet. For the moment, I couldn't feel a thing, so the first thoughts that jumped into my head were *Am I crippled? Did I snap my neck when I hit the ground? Where are my lucky kneepads?*

I tried to move my legs—and the moment I did move it felt as if a thousand knives had suddenly plunged into my flesh.

Well, at least I wasn't paralyzed, and that was great news. But I also knew that I was in some serious trouble.

"DON'T TRY TO MOVE," I was told emphatically by a concerned nurse. "*Just relax.*"

*Relax?* I was beginning to panic. *What happened? Why am I here? Was anyone else hurt? And what, exactly, is wrong with me?*

I think I may have blurted out all of those questions in succession when the head nurse appeared, placed her hand on my forehead, and looked directly at me. I knew what she was doing, something I'd often done myself as an EMT when a patient was on the verge of a breakdown. The human response of touch and eye contact is almost a miracle; it never fails to help calm a panicked victim of an accident.

Then she spoke. "Dan. You've been in an accident and have suffered third- and possibly fourth-degree burns on much of your lower body. We're doing everything we can to make you comfortable. The doctor will be in shortly."

And that was it.

*Third- and possibly fourth-degree burns?* I had never heard of *fourth*-degree burns—and I had been a professional emergency medical technician. I looked back down to my legs and could see some of my flesh peeking out. I was expecting it to looked burnt and charred. I then realized that it was steam, not fire, that got me, so I guess I was more lobster than steak: pale and boiled.

While I tried to "relax," things seemed to be moving incredibly quickly. My first instinct was to call my family, but I was told that they had already been contacted. And when I asked about Kinnie and the team, I was told that they had left. *Hours ago.* I was assured I would see everyone soon after the transfer. *Transfer? What transfer?* I needed to be moved to the Parkland Burn Center in Dallas. Immediately. I had known of Parkland and had read about it while I was studying to be an EMT. It wasn't just the best burn center in the state of Texas; it was, arguably, the best burn center in the country.

As I was prepped for the transfer, I began to try to comprehend what had happened and what was happening. Naturally, my first thoughts were *How long is this going to take? Is the rehabilitation going to take a week? A month? A year?* I had planned to go to California for Christmas to see my family; all I could think was that I needed to go. In retrospect, I should have been on my knees in gratitude (if that were possible) that I hadn't been killed, or that the burns weren't even greater than they were. Thankfully, my manhood was still intact and unharmed. Had Kinnie and the team not been able to cut the pressure to the fuel tanks when they did, the exhaust may have, literally, melted my lower legs off. I'm ashamed that just moments after much of my life was spared by the grace of God, I was already plotting my comeback. However, I was quickly snapped back into reality when the first pang of otherworldly pain began to rear its ugly head. For my entire life I had prided myself on what I thought was an incredible threshold for pain. This had been passed down to me from my father, who was wounded in Vietnam. Schlunds do not complain, and they give no credence to their suffering—no matter how severe.

"*Ahhhhhhh!*" I then screamed.

It wasn't one of those yelps that one blurts out after stubbing their toe. It was one of the those embarrassing, bloodcurdling screams reserved for a character in a *Saw* movie.

"*Ahhhhhhhhhhhh!*"

Suddenly, I was in otherworldly pain. The monitors went off as my blood pressure and heart rate skyrocketed. And I couldn't stop.

"*Ahhhhhhhhhhhhhhhhhhhhhh!*"

Then, I was once again given a reason to be grateful to God. And this time, as the pain quickly subsided and I faded away, I thanked him.

For morphine.

---

Parkland Memorial Hospital is one of the oldest and most famous hospitals in the country. The original hospital opened May of 1894 and operated out of a wooden cabin built on seventeen acres at the corner of Oak Lawn and Maple Avenues in Dallas. The name of the hospital actually comes from what this land had been used for. It was a park. In 1954, Parkland moved to where it is today, at 5200 Harry Hines Boulevard, about a mile from its original site. A year later, the hospital opened its famed burn unit. While Parkland is known for being one of the premier health centers in the world, the hospital is most famous for three individuals who either died or were pronounced dead there: former president John F. Kennedy, his assassin Lee Harvey Oswald, and *his* assassin Jack Ruby.

Prior to arriving at Parkland, I had only a rudimentary knowledge of burns and how to treat them. Of course, I had been witness to some pretty horrific accidents during my time as an EMT, but I had limited experience with burn victims. And the burns that I had treated were only minor. But it didn't take me long to learn how widespread and truly devastating burning was to its victims. Because as horrible as my accident was, with third-degree burns on a wide swath of my buttocks and right thigh, it was still minor compared to some of the patients I saw at Parkland.

If anything, my treatment at Parkland certainly put things into perspective for my own recovery. And while mine was sure to be a long, grueling, and painful period, I couldn't help but be grateful that it wasn't worse. However, I still hadn't realized how life-threatening my injury was. It wasn't the burned skin in itself, it was the risk of infection. The doctor told me much later that patients with such devastating skin damage often don't survive such a large area of missing skin. My new goal was to simply listen to the doctors, do exactly what I was told, and work extra hard during my rehab. I figured if I did all of this, I would get to go home to California for Christmas, which was only three months away. But as week after week passed, it was clear that this was not going to happen.

It is often said in cases of injury and recovery that it's the "mental" aspect of rehabilitation that is the most challenging for a patient. It is incredibly difficult to maintain a positive outlook as progress comes at a snail's pace and sometimes with steps backward. It's said that it's hard not to be impatient or that you have to do things to keep your mind occupied: read, pray, do puzzles. Let me tell you, from my personal experience?—that is 100 percent false. Because for me, nothing can ever come close to describing the overwhelming, furiously angry, explosive pain that I experienced as a burn victim. It is a pain like no other. With third-degree burns, the top layers of your skin are completely gone, leaving only the nerves totally exposed. So sensitive are these nerves that everything and anything causes pain. The slightest breeze feels like a cheese grater shaving at your flesh. Protective gauze feels like sandpaper on an open wound. And topical ointments feel like molten lava spread by a cleaver. And the pain also resonates too. It occupies the inside of your body, pulsating its torment in waves that even my morphine drip couldn't stop. Doctors called it "breakthrough" pain. And it doesn't let up. In fact, if anything, the pain gets worse before it gets better. I can't tell you how many countless hours of sleepless nights I spent in agonizing torture. After a time, the next step was to cover the exposed tissue. Eventually, the cover would be made from skin grafts from my own left leg, but in the interim, it would be "cadaver skin." It wasn't holding well and didn't cover much. As I writhed in pain that radiated through the dead person's skin covering my legs, I decided they could give me boredom all day instead of this.

Eventually, I was released to the care of Kinnie, who took me into his home so I could gather enough strength for the multiple surgeries I would have to undergo. Kinnie put me up in his spare bedroom in his and the doctor's belief that the home environment would be better than Parkland. His reason was psychological, but there was also the fear that my injury was more prey to a staph infection at Parkland than it would be at his home. Whatever the reason, I cannot thank Kinnie and his family enough for this. It's tough enough for a husband and wife living together with their own children to throw a grown and needy man into the equation. Kinnie not only boarded me, but every night he scrubbed my burns to remove the dead skin. And while he did, though I wanted to scream in pain, I kept it in, biting down into a towel with all my might to keep myself quiet. After the tortuous scrub-down, Kinnie lathered my leg with Silvadene, a cream designed for burns that was impervious to bacteria. Once the Silvadene was on, I popped a couple of hydrocodone and waited for just a little of the pain slip away. And as it did, I would say my prayers and find a position of peace. As I would eventually fade into sleep, I would also give thanks to God for Kinnie. Because what he did was above and beyond what any friend could have done.

My time with Kinnie and his family lasted for roughly two weeks, I think; it's hard to remember much because of the amount of painkillers that were flowing through my bloodstream. The time came for me to return to Parkland and begin what would be a series of skin graft surgeries. I had my mom come out for the first surgery because after all, when you're sick or injured you always want your mommy to be around regardless of your age. Though my dad offered, I told him to stay at home because I didn't want him to worry.

I didn't really know what to expect for the skin graft surgery. I knew it would be painful afterwards, but I had no idea what was really taking place. I guess the easiest way to describe it was that the doctors were going to scrape a layer of healthy skin from my left leg and try to attach it to the area that had been burnt during my crash. Regardless of what or how they were doing it, I certainly wasn't looking forward to the surgery.

I woke up incredibly lightheaded and with a Foley catheter attached to my privates (that was my biggest complaint at the time). I was told that the graft went well but I had lost two pints of blood during the surgery. *That doesn't sound good.* And I was given the strict instructions to remain on my side and rest as much as I could. It was advice that was confusing to me. It's not like I was planning to play tennis later that day. But in my postoperative drug-induced haze I nodded and fell back to sleep. A few hours later I woke up on my back and my new skin was, literally, sticking to the sheets and coming off. Today, I still have the worst scars from the missing skin. And oh, for the record, they attached the skin with staples—thirty plus, like a corporate manual.

Flash forward to a week later of me in unbearable pain and making my mother's life absolutely miserable before things got even worse. I knew it the moment it began to happen. As an EMT I knew well the odor of infection. Its pungent smell is distinct—and it needs to be—because it's nature's way of warning you that something is wrong. Kinnie immediately contacted Baylor University Medical Center, and they sent a plastic surgeon named Dr. Zigler to review my situation. The doctor's bedside manners were among the best I'd ever experienced, the perfect combination of kindness and unvarnished honesty.

After studying my wound closely, the doctor's prognosis wasn't good. "I think you should be staying at the hospital, with me. This could be dangerous." He understated the situation.

I told him that I appreciated his help but that I would think about it. I know this seems like a no-brainer, but after being on morphine for months and undergoing a serious surgery, my mind was a blur of confusion, pain, and, most importantly, fear. And I did not want to go to another hospital. I kept thinking of all those convalescent homes I had gone to while I was an EMT and how depressing they were. And I kept picturing myself ending up at one of them and just being left there to die. I guess this was the "mental" part of the accident I would have to face down. And yes, it was tough to think with a clear head at times, as it was extremely so in this moment. But I'd still take Dr. Zigler's and everyone else's advice despite all the fear, skin scraping, grafts, and catheters. So with added encouragement from my mom and Kinnie, I moved to Baylor University Medical Center.

---

Moving to Baylor University Medical Center proved to be one of the best decisions I had ever made—more truthfully, the best *advice* I had ever taken. Of course it makes total sense now. A patient should want to go wherever they have the best chance to recover. At a hospital you have 24-hour care. Yes, it's depressing as hell. Yes, you are alone most of the time. And yes, the food is horrible. But for me, who not only wanted to recover but to regain my strength and return to normal life, I needed to be in a private hospital.

While the decision to move back into another hospital was the good and right one, it did not make my rehabilitation process any shorter or less painful. It just made it more survivable. And in many ways, it also made the process more difficult, because at a hospital, you are just a patient. At Kinnie's house, I was treated as both patient *and* friend. And my mother, who had exactly zero nursing skills, treated me with a loving hand. I was both patient *and* her son. But at a hospital, to even the kindest staff you are nothing more than a patient. And this would play out for me at times in the most uncomfortable ways. For instance, on the days of my bath I felt like a slab of beef getting ready to be processed. I was practically slid onto a cold metal table, naked, as they used an industrial-grade hose to wash me. My skin scraping may have well been done via assembly line, each orderly or nurse as indifferent as the next. And while many of the orderlies performed their mundane jobs with joy, dropping off meals with a smile and a hello, or cleaning the rooms with a pep in their step to improve the mood, in most cases, throughout the day it was business as usual. They simply did their jobs. And when the patient didn't have anything to do with that particular job, they were simply ignored.

I can't say that I was "living my life" at the time. In fact, I can't even say I was surviving. Like the nurses and staff who took care of me, I too just began going through the motions of my "job." And my job was just to not die or lose my mind. That's it. I just wanted to get through the process. To that end, I went through two more surgeries and was nearly catatonic in the process. I said no words as they described the procedure both times, including how and where they would scrape more skin from my good leg and adhere it to my injured one. And I said no words as they cleaned me, blasting me with their hose in the unit's washroom. And I said nothing as they pulled old gauze to replace with new gauze, sometimes taking new or old skin with it.

Four months later, I appeared a different man. Because I hadn't been able to walk, my entire lower body had atrophied. The rest of me was weak and jaundiced. My hair was long and my face had something that resembled a mustache and beard, though it was too patchy to say with certainty. I had also become closed off to the outside world. My steady stream of visitors between Kinnie and the team and my mom had become a trickle. And I had no interest in talking to anyone on the phone. All I did was lay in bed, watch TV, and try to eat when they brought me food. I'm not going to lie, I was in an incredibly bad place both physically and, more importantly, spiritually. I had gotten to feel sorry for myself again. I was angry that rehab was taking so long. I was angry at the quality of the food at the hospital. I was angry at the size of my room. The bad television reception. One especially bitchy night nurse. The smell of the place. I was angry at *everything*. But there was nothing I was angrier at than myself. *Why the hell didn't I kill that throttle sooner? Why couldn't I just land like I had a hundred times before?* I relived the final moments of that last untethered flight in my mind for hours and weeks and months. And the more I did, the deeper removed I became. It got so bad that I actually looked forward to the whirlpool treatments, because at least the soothing water was the only true relief I had during my otherwise drab days.

In due time, I was healed enough to stand, but after being in bed for months on end I could barely walk to the door without huffing and puffing and in excruciating pain. As time passed, though, and with Kinnie's constant persistence in getting me walking, I endured. I knew I would make it.

Not long after that, I was able to walk to the nurse's station. Then to the stairs.

On the first day I made it to the top of the stairs I remember imagining what it may have been like as an infant toddler after having taken my first steps. I pictured myself as that child, ambling toward my father who was waiting for me with open arms.

After all the surgeries, when it was time to go home, I sat down with the doctor. The doctor told me something that never crossed my mind at the time: I almost died! He said: "When I first saw you in the hospital, I didn't think you were going to make it." He explained, "I had spent so many years in the county burn unit and people with a burn that size usually don't make it. You had a bad infection." I started to tear up as he presented the good news. "But I can tell you all this now, knowing you will be fine."

Then, for what I think may have been the first time in a long, long time, that strange feeling came.

I smiled.

# 10

# Relaunch

After roughly a year of recovery, I will not say that I was a new man. In the end, I had lost over 183 inches of skin. The new skin was peculiar, self-alienating. There was no sensation, and there was no sweat. I would have phantom itching from beneath the skin layer that I couldn't scratch. The skin was never tight or restricting, but my muscles were not initially in coordination—as I once found out when I tried to run across the street, only to fall to my knees.

I thought of the whole experience like buying a new car: Expect to get scratches and have accidents. My life was to be lived and not sheltered. I had suffered greatly but I survived to live another day—something I attributed to God. Deep down I knew he had plans for me, I just didn't know what it was. But even if I was never told, I was thankful for my injury. It turned me into the man I am today.

But I did have one apprehension: Who will love me with this scar?

I would say I was a renewed man. Everyone who has come out of the darkness emerges with a different perspective on life. For some, the perspective is secular and pragmatic. They have ruminated on what has happened and have gained the knowledge and experience so as to avoid what placed them in that spot. Some emerge with a spiritual perspective like me. They take the experience as an act of God, using it as a springboard to make a second lease on life. And others? Well, unfortunately, many don't ever leave the darkness. It remains a part of them for the rest of their lives. I think that I came out of my accident as all three of the above.

By nature, I have always been pragmatic, thoughtful. If I wanted to do something, I would figure it out, whether it meant asking the right people or studying the topic. Everything in life had a code that could be broken. To that end, I knew that there was nothing metaphysical about what had happened to me. I made a very simple mistake on my last untethered flight. The issue wasn't training; it wasn't equipment or crew. There were consequences to that mistake that were much greater than what I was prepared for. I knew that now. And I knew I would never be anything shy of 100 percent prepared for anything I attempted in the future. As far as the spiritual aspect of my accident, while I may have complained and grumbled and even cursed at God for the pain and suffering I was enduring, I never once questioned His hand in it all. I prayed for healing, but sometimes you have to thank God for your experiences in life, even if He never gives you a reason. I knew there was a reason, but I didn't know what it was. God has always been with me—even when I ignored Him. He was always by my side when I was soaring through the air before my crash. And He was with me in my darkest nights alone during my recovery. So, from a spiritual perspective, my feeling was the same both before and after the accident.

He's got a plan.

---

One of His plans was to introduce Shannon Gibson into my life. Shannon is Kinnie's younger brother and he had been with the Rocketman organization from the beginning with Kinnie. He started attending jobs with us. I suspect Kinnie saw it as a way to keep an honest eye on me and my performances, but Shannon and I hit it off like brothers from another mother. He was not only uniquely insightful of the mechanics of the Rocketbelt, but even without ever having flown it himself he had a natural understanding of a pilot's performance and quickly became my "flight director." He was there for all my triumphs and my failures. He was my confidant in an industry that only a handful could understand. I had found a true friend.

As for coming out of the darkness, I can't say that I didn't take a little of it with me when I left. Before my accident, I had been practically invincible. I had jumped off thirty-foot scaffolds. I had dived off of speeding boats. I was a licensed pyrotechnician, advanced scuba diver, and experienced EMT. I had been engulfed in flames a thousand times, fallen on cars and crashed into walls. But I had never suffered anything more serious than a twisted ankle or a bruised arm. The Rocketbelt accident didn't just severely injure my legs, rendering me an invalid for months; it was a gutshot to my impervious ego that as a stuntman I was, in fact, not invincible. As a result, I carried that accident with me for the rest of my career and even to this day. It is a part of me that I cannot let go of. And to be perfectly honest, it has hampered me in some ways. After the accident, I was never quite as aggressive in my flights as I'd been before. This is why I never reached the pinnacle of my flight ability. I was, perhaps, too meticulous in my training and preparation. There is something good to be said about caution, but when it comes to flight and performance, there is also an aspect of improvisation that should be in the equation. It's due perhaps to my new rigidness that I became slightly less dynamic during performances.

Yet it also kept me alive. And safe.

But I wanted more. I wanted to push my limits.

And yet again, when I wanted to try something extra, Shannon would often say, "Do the flight, get the check, and let's go home." Deep down, I think I was grateful he was there to tell me this.

And I knew that, in the end, I was also grateful for the new sense of caution my accident inspired in me.

---

Strapping back on the Rocketbelt had always been my plan—at least one more time. It may have not been the plan of my family or friends or even Kinnie and his team, but from the moment I woke up in that hospital bed in McKinney, it was my plan. Still, it came as a surprise to almost everyone when I expressed that I was going to return to flying.

I still wanted to be a Rocketman.

The strength of my desire to get back into the Rocketbelt surprised even myself, because it turned out that the very day before my crash and burn, I'd had the opportunity to chat with a living legend in the Rocketman community.

Hal Graham was the first man to ever fly a Rocketbelt. He was nicknamed "His Eminence" for being the Neil Armstrong of our small world. Hal was happy to hear about my successful free flights, and we even discussed the possibility of working together some day. But mostly, we had that long conversation about the life of a Rocketman that led to us talking about what made Hal stop flying. As he explained, there is really only one reason a Rocketman ceases to fly: He crashes. That's it. It was a curious response to what I would discover is a very esoteric question. I mean, there has to be more moving parts to it, *right*? There has to be a logical, physical, or perhaps even a spiritual aspect as to why a Rocketman quits flying. But now that I think back on it, Hal's answer to that question could not have been more accurate. Because as I would discover in due time, when it came to hanging up my Rocketbelt, it wasn't because I got too old or too heavy (though that would come in due time). It wasn't because I had become a husband and a father. And it wasn't because I wanted to leave the lifestyle of a Rocketman behind. I eventually quit flying for the same reason Rocketmen usually quit flying and for the same reason Hal Graham did. *I crashed.*

Most people have a pretty good understanding of the word "crashed." The word has obvious physical connotations and we've all had accidents of one sort or another. But while there is a physical aspect to the word, there is also a figurative meaning. It has come to be a metaphor for a "falling from grace" or hitting "rock bottom." And this too is something almost all of us experience. A marriage can crash. A business can crash. And we can crash in other ways too. We all fall short of the glory of God and so many of us battle with the demons of drugs or alcohol or other vices. And all of these can cause a much more consequential crash than just physical injury. However, for the Rocketman, the word "crash" carries both definitions simultaneously. It is a fall from the sky—and a fall from grace. It is a collision course to Earth and its waiting realities, and also a collision with one's own spirit.

My return to Kinnie's hangar wasn't exactly like Odysseus's return from Troy. I just returned to my previous mundane tasks of making fuel and managing shows—very business as usual. Kinnie and his team couldn't have been more welcoming. They immediately brought me back into their fold and made me feel as if I hadn't been gone a day. However, I did get a sense that nobody wanted to talk about the elephant in the room. I know it may have had something to do with aviation culture, or maybe they were afraid to step on any nerves, but nobody said anything about my last flight. It was as if it was part of the job. And it was. But though I wasn't ready to go back up just yet, it was clear that I was determined to fly again. Thankfully, it was clear to Kinnie too. Having invested over $100,000 in me as a Rocketman, he wanted to see it through. But Kinnie also knew something that I hadn't known: Injury was simply a part of the Rocketbelt journey. He had experienced a serious crash himself, almost losing his left foot several years before I joined the team. Eric had crashed, too, tearing out his rotator cuff and blowing out both his knees. Heck, they *all* had crashed. So, getting back in the Rocketbelt was something a true Rocketman did. I was not going to be the exception. I was not going to go back to California a failure. I was not going to live with a scar on my legs only to say I gave up. Most importantly, I was pissed off, so I was going to go back up. At least one more time! If only to prove to myself that I ended on a high note.

Sheri was the only one who finally broached what I guess was supposed to be a very sensitive subject.

"Well," she said. "Are you sure about this, Dan?"

"I wouldn't be here if I wasn't," I said.

"At least you got it out of the way," she said.

"Got what out of the way?" I asked.

"An accident. Every pilot has one. Now you'll be good to go."

I guess that was one good way of looking at it.

---

It was eerie to return to the scene of my accident. And though I am not a superstitious person, it was tough to stand on the same spot where I had crashed and wondered if it had been cursed. Still, it was the first place I went when I returned to the hangar. I wanted to stand in that exact spot that I almost died and take a moment to think. I wasn't contemplating the accident which

I had played out in my mind in a loop for what seemed over a year—that was already burned into my consciousness. At this moment, on this spot, I wanted to rethink all I had survived to *return* here. I thought of the unbearable pain, the sleepless nights, the morphine daze, the skin scrapes, the surgeries, the catheters, the bad food, and the aloneness of it all. I had survived *all* of that.

*Could it happen again?*

As I stood there staring at the spot, a wave of strength washed over me. I was now ready to face my demon, and it wasn't that spot. Just like the stuntman who almost killed himself at that stunt show, I was going to fly again, and I was going to land in the same damn spot, smack-dab on the emotional bloodstain that literally scarred me for life. But there was something else to confront. My demon was locked up in the hangar in the Rocketbelt room.

With a little humor, I told Kinnie that I was going to "have a talk" with the Rocketbelt. I told myself that it would be just like bumping into the kid who used to bully you in junior high school. He may have looked big and scary to you back then, but now he's just a manager at Buffalo Wild Wings. The psychological trope worked. I opened the door, and as dramatic as it sounds, there it was, just propped up on the stand, untouched. And yet it looked even more menacing than it did before. I was confronting my demon.

"You're mine, bitch," I said. Unlike most pieces of equipment that are supposed to assist mankind in some way, the Rocketbelt looked as if it were built to do more harm than good. And unlike me, it also looked impervious to destruction. I stood there for a long time, staring at the machine that had nearly killed me, leaving my body forever patched together and scarred. It didn't even have a scratch on it. The control arms had bent a bit and it looked like it could use a good cleaning, but it was still in perfect working order. It pissed me off. As I stared at the Rocketbelt, an idea came to mind: It was *missing* something.

I went to Kinnie and shared my idea. He told me it wasn't necessary, but if I was going to be the pilot I had some say in the matter.

So at the valve/cable attachment on the top of the machine I installed an emergency pull pin that would immediately shut down the Rocketbelt. This way, if what happened to me happened again, the crew would be able to turn the Rocketbelt off much faster.

---

When it came time to go back up, I was disappointed but not surprised that it would be on the tether. This was a step back for me. I thought I had completed that step. After all, when you fall off a ten-speed you don't restart on a bike with training wheels. But this was my ego talking. The truth was, Kinnie didn't have to retrain me at all. He had already invested an enormous amount of time and capital into my training, only to have me fail. I was actually lucky he even gave me my old job back. However, Kinnie was also a stunt-oriented businessman—and a very good one. The truth was, I was an excellent pilot candidate. And despite my slow learning curve and subsequent crash, another pilot on the team would effectively double his income. So there were also professional reasons for him to be vested in my success. Like any good businessman, he needed to protect his investment. And that meant that the smart play was to cable me up until I was ready again.

After a year of not being strapped up, I hadn't realized how good it would feel to be attached to a Rocketbelt again. I loved the feel of its weight on my back. And I missed how comforting it was to have the buckles pulled as tightly as they could. Usually, the toughest thing for me as a pilot-in-training was that once I was strapped up, the wait before going up was excruciating. Sometimes I would have to walk around for fifteen minutes lugging the Rocketbelt with me as the team prepped the cables and covered all their other pre-launch responsibilities. But being strapped up for the first time since the accident, I relished every second of the wait. And if anything, I was the one who prolonged the practice flight, meandering around the hangar and tinkering with my suit.

The actual flight on the cable was anticlimactic. It was, after all, tethered, so there was little chance of injury. The only question left to be answered was *Can I still do it?*

The answer was a resounding YES.

"Just like riding a bike"—I know this is a rather cliché expression used to describe restarting an endeavor, but the sentiment held true for me with the Rocketbelt. The moment I lifted off, everything came back to me: my sense of balance, my focus, my feel for the throttle. I knew that I had been getting better at flying the Rocketbelt, but I really didn't know I was *that* good. In a matter of moments, I realized I'd completed my first hop since the accident, and I had done it as easily as if I had been asked to park a car.

We did one or two more tethered flights before it became clear that I really no longer needed them. Not long after that, Kinnie had me strap up for my first free flight since the accident with the understanding that if I bounce, don't touch me. Success! One flight turned into two, two into four, four into eight, and before I knew it, I was learning to make turns, ascending to great heights, and even nailing the elusive pirouette.

As 2004 came to a close, it was all but official. I had shown Kinnie, the team, and most of all myself that I was indeed a smart investment—I had become a qualified Rocketbelt pilot but not yet a Rocketman. And the following year, I would show the rest of the world.

# PART THREE

# Birth of a Rocketman

Let perseverance finish its work so that you may be mature and complete, not lacking anything.

—James 1:4

# 11

# Takeoff

On July 25, 2005, I made my professional debut in Miami, where they were hosting the MTV Music Video Awards. We were hired to do a promotion in which rapper Sean "P. Diddy" Combs was supposed to arrive at a press conference via Rocketbelt. Obviously, there was a sleight of hand involved and I was going to be the pilot who flew over the presser, then land behind the stage where P. Diddy would come out wearing an identical suit and holding my helmet. It was a simple flight and perfect for my first job. But it was also the first time I had ever flown the Rocketbelt anywhere other than Kinnie's hangar.

A day before the press conference, the team and I gathered for a test run with the network. While there, I met the MTV brass, production staff, and P. Diddy himself, who seemed to be there with at least twenty members of his entourage. When introduced to Diddy he looked at me sideways.

"Yo, I don't know. If we can't make it look real . . ." he said. "If it ain't believable, I don't want to do it."

Obviously, he was pointing out the fact that he and I look nothing alike. P. Diddy is Black; I'm white as a chalk. But I said to him, "Look, Mr. Diddy, all we need to do is add some black makeup to my hands; and the face shield is already tinted, so nobody will not know the difference."

I don't know if it was what I said or how I said it, but it looked like whichever it was, it offended Diddy. He stared at me as if I were an idiot.

"I'm not really black," he said. "I'm more of a . . . chocolate brown."

I didn't know if he was kidding or if I had legitimately offended him, so I just kind of smiled, shrugged and said, "Mr. Diddy, I can do whatever color you'd like."

He thought about it for a moment before his face bent into a huge smile.

"That's all I need to hear, my man," he said.

We then prepared to do the test flight—but before we started, something happened that I did not expect. I became *incredibly* anxious. I don't know what it was. Maybe it was the travel. Maybe it was the scorching Miami heat. Maybe it was the strange environment, but all of a sudden, I was a nervous wreck. And just as sudden, the platform I was set to take off from seemed incredibly small. Not to mention there was a row of palm trees blocking me from seeing my landing "spot." On top of everything, Diddy and his entire entourage were watching me like a science experiment. I then overheard one of them say, "This shit is crazy. These dudes crash all the time."

*Are they expecting a crash? Are they* hoping *for a crash?*

Usually before I take off I pump myself up to build confidence, but suddenly I felt like the coyote strapped to the Acme rocket. Once the doubt began to creep in, it kind of snowballed from there and I nearly had a bona fide panic attack. I desperately wanted to be anywhere but there. What was I thinking? I missed my old job at Six Flags. I missed my old responsibility as Managing Director. Hell, I missed being an EMT. On paper, being P. Diddy's body double while flying a Rocketbelt to a press conference for a glamorous awards show in Miami Beach, well, that sounded great. But was it really? I wondered.

Just as I was on the cusp of losing it, though, I refocused and brought myself back. I had worked too hard for this. I had experienced too much. The moment belonged to me. I reminded myself that I was well-trained, well-honed, and had a great team behind me. I was qualified! It was what I was born for. So I prayed up, stepped onto the platform, and turned the throttle.

Walk. In. The. Park.

Well, almost. It turned out I flew straight into a palm tree, but the thrust from my Jetovators simply pushed the palm branches out of the way, and I passed unscathed.

And when the actual event took place the next day, I did even better. I overshot the palm trees by a good fifteen feet, spun around, and flew backwards for a bit before completing a textbook landing. In fact, so good was my flight, a photo of it even made its way into *People* Magazine (though Diddy got the credit). After the press conference, I tracked down Diddy and told him, "Hey, you looked great up there!" He agreed. I was thrilled—the role of the Rocketman is not just to perform an exciting flight but to make the client look good! It was a great event and one of the cooler gigs I'd get to do. (Of course, no one could've predicted then the amount of trouble in which the artist would find himself in recent years. Fortunately, I was never witness to his exploits outside of our preparations and our performance for him.)

With my first professional flight complete, it was official: I was now a Bona Fide Rocketman! In fact, after that maiden flight, Kinnie and the team presented me with a beautiful plaque titled "Order of Rocketmen." It read:

> *Let it be known to all men that on the twenty-fifth day of July in the year of our Lord 2005 that the honoree below earned the right and title of Rocketman. From this day forward may all that know address him as such!*

And it had my name etched into it at the bottom. It was one of the proudest achievements of my life.

---

My next gig was at the Melbourne Royal Show in Australia, and my job was nothing more than a simple demonstration of the Rocketbelt. It was the perfect show for a blossoming pilot: twenty-two flights spread over eleven days straight with two flights per day. I just had to say a few words, take off, fly a couple hundred feet, and land. Then, after each show I had to spend about thirty minutes visiting VIPs, signing autographs, and taking pictures. It was like being paid to practice. As simple as this was, however, it was here that I suffered my first professional hiccup.

Sometimes, the easiest performances are the toughest ones. Think of it this way: Most accidents don't happen on the freeways where cars drive incredibly fast and you have to constantly check your mirrors and think before you make any kind of move. Anyone with years of driving experience understands that most accidents take place in the parking lot of a Walmart or when picking up your kids from school when they're not paying attention to the smaller details of the space around them, and the outcome is usually no more than a little fender bender. Point is: It's easy for us to pay even *less* attention on the freeways. The Rocketbelt is no different in this respect. Doing a simple thing like taking off, flying for fifty yards, and then turning and landing was pretty easy for me. Naturally, it was so easy that on one flight I miscalculated my elevation as I descended and ended up landing on my knees. It wasn't a real big deal, but it was embarrassing. Afterwards, I told the crowd, "I like to end my flights the way I start them—on my knees praying." They all got a kick out of it.

Kinnie was brilliant for starting me out with low-level events. I don't mean to demean them in any way, because they were all awesome. But they weren't the high-profile stadium events that were the business's bread and butter. The jobs I went on were cornflakes: easy to put up, easy to go down. And best for Kinnie, they were lucrative. With two Rocketmen on the team, Kinnie could now put more effort into landing those high-profile events. He would never again lose money, because now he could never be overbooked. Prior to my promotion to Rocketman, Eric did all the flying. He did the huge, glam performances, but he also did the smaller ones. And sometimes when he was booked for a smaller one, a really sizable event would sprout up, but Kinnie couldn't take it. As a principled businessman, he would never cancel a job if a better one came along. Well, now with me on board he would never have that problem again. We had two Rocketbelts and two pilots. He could take *all* of them . . .

If only Eric hadn't soon moved on to do other things.

Once my Rocketman career began, I began to sense that it was taking on a life of its own. And this is something that I thought might happen. But I was also convinced that it could never take me with it. I thought that I would exist with two personas. One: Dan Schlund, the grounded, happy-go-lucky kid from California who loved adventure and entertaining people. The other: the Rocketman, the daring, dashing, crowd-pleasing pilot. But flight after flight, country after country, continent after continent, and performance after performance, the latter began to take hold of me. Sadly, this was the last thing I thought that would ever happen—because I could *never* lose my way, could I? Others lose their way. But not people like me. Not people who had parents like mine. Not people who pray every day and have experienced loss and pain and are inherently good and decent people like me. *Right?*

Wrong. In fact, it happens to people *exactly* like me. And ironically—though appropriately—it began with another crash. (Funny how so many life-altering moments are centered around a crash. . . .)

To be clear, while I was capable and professional when it came to flying the Rocketbelt, I was not a "great" pilot. Eric was a great pilot. I was a good pilot who was great with people. One of the things that held me back from being a *great* pilot was that I just couldn't maneuver the way Eric could. That guy could make the belt *dance*. Me? I kind of guided the Rocketbelt, massaging it as best I could. And while I had become very adept at making gorgeous and sweeping left turns, I struggled to do the same on the right turns. I was like a NASCAR driver, always going left. Well, on one flight, I tried to go right to correct the over-yaw I had made while turning left. As with a motorcycle I cranked the handles, but unlike a bike, the Rocketbelt requires more finesse, less brute force. The moment I started, I knew it wasn't a good idea, so I figured I'd just straighten out and go left again. But as soon as I did this, I got off-balance. I realized that I might end up flying right over the audience, which was an absolute no-no for reasons I've mentioned, so I went back into another right turn to correct my imbalance. Suddenly, I found myself spinning out of control and falling toward the ground. I had been in dozens of spins over the years, but they were always on the tether. As soon as they started, Kinnie or his staff would always wrangle me in. I had assumed any correction would lead to a horrible and violent crash—but I wasn't *absolutely* certain. So, I stayed calm, held my spin so as not to endanger the public, and I watched the ground get closer as it spiraled toward me. It was hard to get my bearings; I was in a "death spiral," but I did the best I could and the closer I got to the ground I just thought to myself, *Well, here comes the boom!*

And boy, did it come.

I landed smack-dab on my stomach, but was shielded from much of the collision by the control arms. Granted, I was also crushed by the hundred-plus pounds of metal on my back, but the safety crew was on top of me in an instant. Bill Reed, one of our best technicians who was with me during most of my training, quickly pulled the emergency-pin release I had installed and shut the machine off. The safety straps were released and I rolled out.

I couldn't know what the crash looked like from a spectator point of view. I'm sure it looked awful, but I could feel the entire audience waiting with bated breath to see if I was okay. In the moment I thought I could've had a broken back for all I knew, I was in so much pain. But still, I did what any good stunt performer does when they suffer a fall or crash: I popped up and gave two big thumbs-up before jogging away to applause.

Back in our trailer, the Rocketbelt and I were assessed for damage. Naturally, the Rocketbelt was mostly fine (it always was) except for the bent control arms. As far as I was concerned, nothing broken, just a really sore back. What *really* hurt was my bruised ego. The crash could not have happened at a worse time because I had really begun to build back confidence as a pilot. So I sulked in my trailer for a long time afterward. Staff would come by with fans or friends of our client, but I shooed them away. Finally, Shannon stopped by. I couldn't shoo *him* away. As both Kinnie's brother and my flight director, he was, after all, my right-hand man and confidant. He walked in, sat down across from me, and just stared at me. And I couldn't even bring myself to stare back. Instead, I just broke down and started crying. He gave me a moment before he finally spoke.

"Dan," he said. "What's wrong?"

"I don't think I can do this," I said. "I keep crashing. I'm going to call Kinnie and quit."

Shannon didn't skip a beat.

"No you're not, Dan."

I looked up at him, surprised at how direct he was. He then went on.

"Dan, you are doing things on this Rocketbelt that no new pilot has ever done. You're doing sweeping turns and pirouettes. So you had a crash, big fucking deal. But you know *what? You even sold that!* The way you popped up afterward. The crowd loved it."

I hadn't thought about it, but it was a good save.

He continued, "Dan, you have what it takes, because being a Rocketman is more than just being able to fly the belt."

Those words really resonated with me and still do today. *Being a Rocketman is more than just being able to fly the belt.* It *was* true, after all. Obviously, being able to fly was a prerequisite, but being a Rocketman required so many other things, the first of which being resilience, followed by an ability to stay calm in an emergency. It was in that moment that Shannon became not just my flight director and quasi-boss, but my best friend. His words helped me forge a self-confidence that I needed at the time—despite that it would eventually lead me down a very selfish path. But for now, I felt fantastic. With Shannon's stamp of approval, I now thought of myself as a true Rocketman. And from that moment on, for better and for worse, *I would act like it.*

The crew stayed up all night fixing the belt, and I went to massage therapy.

The next day we were up flying again. It wasn't easy and quite painful, but we fulfilled the contract with no further issues.

# 12

# In the Band

With my first few gigs as a professional Rocketman under my belt and that confidence-shaking second crash behind me, I quickly fell into a rhythm. I liken it to being on tour with a rock 'n' roll band. We booked out a year. We rehearsed. Then we hit the road, doing a number of shows in Europe, then shot over to Asia for a few more before returning home and doing shows throughout the United States, beginning on the East Coast and finishing on the West. Before I knew it I had over a million frequent-flier miles and needed more visa pages in my passport. As mentioned, I had toured with the team before as their operations manager, so I thought I had an idea of what to expect, but as I quickly learned, it is much different being a part of the crew than being one of its featured performers. Again, to use the band analogy, it's one thing to be the road manager of The Rolling Stones, but it's an entirely different experience to be Mick Jagger. Now, I wasn't just "with the band," I was its lead singer.

As Kinnie had hoped when he trained me, his investment had paid off big time, because just like the Rocketbelt itself, his business took off. More appearances meant more exposure. And more exposure meant more flight requests. But the number of requests Kinnie received was something even Kinnie couldn't have predicted. Not only was he profiting from the venues themselves as our rates continually rose, he received even more exposure from the buzz they created. A flight with the Rocketbelt seemed to enliven every region where we did a show. It is still incredible to me how people are enamored with the idea of self-propelled flight. No matter how big the venue or how special the occasion, everyone would stop what they were doing and watch our flight. And not only did we get the full attention of those we performed in front of, local news crews often showed up at venues—not for the act or the promotion, but to actually cover our flight. We made newspapers and were asked to go on radio shows, and as a result Kinnie's phone wouldn't stop ringing. Some of the requests were crazy. We were asked to fly for marriages at the Henry Ford Plantation, perform at bar mitzvahs in Turkey, and show up at motorcycle rallies in Canada. We were even asked to do a political flight against the president of Venezuela; at the time we didn't make the connection that he was a dictator and that we could've gotten killed doing it. It was only by the grace of God that we weren't arrested and somehow made it home.

As I flew more, my confidence and skill steadily improved. And while I still managed all the shows and handled visas, shipping, and logistics, flying was now my passion and I considered myself a pilot first. However, Kinnie had become busy with other ventures and wasn't around as much for shows, so I once again put on my "boss" hat. Overall, I didn't mind managing the shows I performed in. I didn't like the responsibility of dealing with the clients and logistics of any given show, but it was the only way to be sure it was done my way, and I was the only one who could do it all. I felt that the added responsibility diminished my joy of flying because it made it feel like a business, and unfortunately, I was put into this position far more often than I liked. Before my piloting days, my experience was that *everything* was business, so it was a relief to just be a pilot. Now I understood how difficult it had been for Kinnie when he was both flying and running the business himself. Because whenever I was forced to wear those two hats, I was faced with a choice of what was right for me as a Rocketman, and what was best for the Rocketman brand.

Nevertheless, while having to manage the business of it all, I was at least glad that I could do it *my* way.

A very common conflict in managing the business was clients making last-minute requests that the Rocketman was to carry something while performing. This could be a logo affixed to the suit or helmet or maybe even a banner tied to the Rocketbelt. Because these requests were so common, I had drawn up a technical rider for the clients as to what we could or could not carry, what we could take off from, and also what was required as far as our preparation. Obviously, some things posed a flight risk. The length and weight of even a small flag has an effect on wind drag, propulsion, and balance. Theoretically, it could also get caught on something. I've had flights where I had to clear trees or had landings where I had to descend into the small confines of a scaffold. *Anything* can happen. And there is no time to "go around" for a second approach. Despite these risks, I rarely said no to a request. As a Rocketman, I felt as if it were part of my duty; but as a businessman, I probably should have been more prudent. This would almost end up biting me in the backside at a show we were supposed to do in Vienna, Austria.

Austria had always been one of my favorite countries—even before I became a Rocketman. *The Sound of Music* was one of my dad's favorite films, and as a child I had always wanted to visit the setting. I daydreamed of romping around like the Von Trapp kids, hiking its mountains and playing in Salzburg. Needless to say I was over the moon when we booked a job in Austria for the cosmetic company L'Oréal. It was a big job for us with a very high-profile brand and a good number of celebrities, models, and politicians expected to be in attendance. The pilot's task was to show up at the event, then fly from the red carpet and land on a ten-foot-high stage to present a plaque to the mayor. This was elementary. However, when it came time for the event, the circumstances were anything but.

One of the toughest things I discovered as a Rocketman is that you are never allowed to have a bad day. This goes without saying for the actual performance. The flight itself has to be perfect. It is, after all, a matter of life and death. But as Shannon had told me, there was more to the Rocketman than just the belt. The Rocketman is not just a performer, he's a persona. He must be engaging and enthusiastic. He must manifest wish fulfillment on behalf of his audiences. And for the most part, this was always one of my greatest strengths. Say what you want about my right turns or occasional shoddy landings, I was a people pleaser. I loved smiling for the camera and running into the audience after a flight to shake hands with fans. I never said no to a photo, an autograph, or a hug. It was truly the best thing about being a Rocketman. But I was human too. And humans have bad days. And for a variety of reasons while I was in Austria—travel fatigue, jet lag, a sinus infection, missing my family—I just wasn't in a good place. Naturally, L'Oréal asked for an odd request: to affix a rather sizable replica of one of their iconic lipstick containers on the back of my belt. And naturally, I said yes.

My approval of L'Oréal's request was foolish on two fronts. First, I could feel that my balance was off. I don't know why but I just didn't feel right. And secondly, the replica lipstick was too heavy. I should have known this immediately, but my ego wouldn't allow it. Even Shannon advised against it but I overruled him. It was only during my practice flight that I would find out the hard way. After a wonky takeoff and wobbly flight, I landed on the edge of the stage they had built, and the additional weight of the stupid lipstick prop drew me backwards—and I fell off the platform, plummeting ten feet and landing on my shoulder. It hurt like hell and, again, I was very lucky it didn't end up worse. Still, I dusted off and we fixed the belt, which only had a bent bracket, and we did another test. This time, I tipped over during takeoff and burned the red carpet. It was kind of a disaster and would be the only event we ever had to cancel. I was especially upset because I was finally in Austria. But I guess God Himself didn't want us to perform. I would have to shelve my childhood fantasies of romping around Salzburg.

But I learned a tough lesson: Say *no.*

My favorite flights never involved carrying anything. They required *wearing* something. As part of the performances we offered, we had specialized suits like tuxedos, Santa suits, and my three favorites: Master Chief from the video game *Halo*, the *Star Wars* stormtrooper Captain Rex, and one of the film's iconic characters, Boba Fett. But these costumes also presented the biggest challenges for me as a pilot. Some were weighty and cumbersome. Others were too tight and decreased my mobility. Both could throw off my balance and timing. But ultimately, the costumes were rendered safe and carefully designed to both conceal the straps and also be "rip ready" in case we needed to get to the emergency-release buckles in the event of a crash. The helmet too would have to be retrofitted. I would personally fashion a bicycle helmet to the inside of each prop helmet, not for safety but so that it stayed on my head as I looked around. I also loved doing costumed flights for another reason: They were usually a really big deal to the crowd and a welcome challenge for me. And whenever the crowd was excited, it rubbed off on me.

One of my most memorable costumed flights was when we headlined an event for the thirtieth anniversary of *Star Wars* at their annual convention in Los Angeles. Being a *Star Wars* fan, I reached out to Lucasfilm and gave a great discount. Obviously, anything related to the *Star Wars* franchise always drew a crowd, and for that event, a large group of fans known as the 501st Legion was to be on hand. They were the most well-known and popular group of *Star Wars* fanboys and fangirls who had made their own costumes and replica weapons with incredible attention to detail. The 501st Legion were so popular they were often asked to do special appearances at hospitals and parades. Needless to say, they took anything *Star Wars* related deathly serious. For the anniversary show, I had to kick off the convention by making a surprise appearance just outside the Staples Center in Los Angeles. To execute this, I had the 501st gather to form a circle around the landing pad, where Darth Vader was awaiting a visitor. I used the 501st because at a *Star Wars* convention, stormtroopers were more respected than the security personnel. Everyone knew someone of great importance was coming. (*But who? Will it be one of the actors? Could it be George Lucas himself?*) In any case, it was going to be a very special moment. The anticipation was palpable.

As planned and practiced, the circle was clear and Darth Vader stood in the middle of it, calm, composed, and as menacing as ever. The stormtroopers stood at attention and all on hand were waiting with building anticipation. Suddenly, an incredibly loud, screaming pitch could be heard. And a moment later, all looked to the sky where, coming in from about a hundred yards away, was Boba Fett (yours truly) flying toward them over the trees. I was pumped with so much adrenaline as I came in for my landing that I did two full pirouettes before sticking one of the best landings I had ever made. And as soon as I did, I could hear the thunderous applause. I then walked over to

Darth Vader and shook his hand before we both walked into the convention together to rousing cheers. It wasn't just a special moment. It was an *epic moment* worthy of the *Star Wars* universe.

Inside the convention, I took countless pictures and even met the actual actor who played Boba Fett. His name was Jeremy Bulloch and he couldn't have been nicer. I signed autographs, spoke to fans, and even made some contacts for future events. However, the gig was not without its controversy. While I was and still am a huge fan of the *Star Wars* universe, I did not take my level of fandom all that seriously. Still, it was expected that while I was at the convention, I should abide by the code of the 501st Legion. The core of that code was that while in character, whether a stormtrooper, Darth Vadar or anyone else, you could never, ever remove your "bucket" (helmet). In other words, I had to stay in character during the show and under no circumstances show my face. Of course, I took off my helmet about ten minutes into the convention and only put it back on for special photo requests. To me, it was no big deal. The way I looked at it, I was the one and only person to actually fly as Boba Fett with a real-life jet pack, so I could do what I wanted. But to some members of the 501st and a small host of fans in that world, I had committed a mortal sin. In fact, I was raked over the coals online after I posted a video of my flight and removal of the helmet—but I didn't care. I wish I could say that I was genuinely contrite, but in all honesty, I wasn't. And I'm still not. But I was reminded of a lesson that I had been taught as a child: You can never truly please everyone. And in all honesty, I was okay with that, because as I continued being the Rocketman, the only person I really wanted to please was myself and the clients (and perhaps George Lucas).

---

After nearly three years of being the Rocketman, I was at the top of my game. I had overcome the physical hurdles of flying the Rocketbelt and had become an excellent pilot. As far as the rest it took to be a Rocketman, I had mastered that in spades. I knew how to work a crowd and please a client better than anyone. But I also embraced the lifestyle, indulging in all the perks that were offered to me. And my behavior, no matter how libertine, always rode on the built-in excuse that I was traveling. Or that I was an itinerant performer. Or just an old-school pilot who went from job to job. And so, like the Rocketbelt itself, my role in every city or country I went to was temporal. Fleeting. I was there to put on a show and leave. That's it. And anyone lucky enough to wade into my orbit could come for the ride—even if it was a short one. I had made many great friends over the years, but it was impossible to keep up with everyone. It was a constant ritual of saying goodbye to good friends and hello to new friends show after show, knowing I might not ever see them again. But here's the thing: Even after thirty-four countries and six continents, after countless parties where I ate some of the most expensive food in the world, drank some of the best liquor, all while taking full advantage of my bachelorhood, I *still* wasn't happy.

It's quite easy to become self-absorbed, especially when you're single, have no children, and are without any real responsibilities outside of fulfilling your own passions. But the thing is, it doesn't happen overnight. Instead, it is something that takes place over time. It can take place over years and years of striving to achieve goals only to replace them with new ones once you've checked them off the list. And naturally, self-absorption comes at the expense of friends and family. Even worse, it comes at the expense of slowly losing yourself and a sense what you were truly meant to be. But the worst of all in the road to self-absorption is that we cannot see it happening. At least I couldn't.

It's hard to pin down when my discontent began, because when I think back on it, it actually may have *always* been there. But as was my state of mind at the time, we often look no further than what will fix the pain in front of us instead of truly asking ourselves what was causing it in the first place. For me, I thought it stemmed from a deep-seated insecurity that made me believe I wasn't good enough. While this can be traced all the way back to my childhood, as a Rocketman it manifested into what became a quest for getting better. I needed to be *the best*. I needed to be the most well-liked. I needed to be the most skilled. I needed to make a positive image for the world to see. If I felt I wasn't, I would put so much pressure on myself to achieve that it drove me crazy. The PTSD I suffered after my first two crashes certainly exacerbated things too. Because even though I was driven, deep inside I was also afraid. I don't know what exactly I was afraid of—I already knew the worst possible outcome. I had already crashed and burned 18 percent of my body. And I knew very well that every time I went up, I could die. It wasn't as if we were just flying thirty feet off the ground. Often, I would hit heights of a hundred feet and in excess of thirty miles per hour—once over eighty miles per hour. As all of this filled my head, I couldn't make up my mind whether to be crippled by the fear or to completely disregard it and just fly. It made me a basket case before flights, though I would never show this outwardly.

Although I'd struggled with this internal turmoil from the very beginning of my ascension as a Rocketman, the anxiety it caused seemed to swell with each event. And though I don't think it affected my performances, it certainly took its toll on me psychologically. I had known that being a Rocketman would be a challenge. But I was not prepared as to how I would cope if I ever began to lose control of who I was. Quietly and privately, I sought therapy in the hopes that it would help, and it did to a certain extent. It was good to share my innermost fears and vent about any frustrations that had been buried within me. But at the end of the day, nothing I shared could do anything to quell my preflight anxiety or quiet the noise in my head that only seemed to grow louder and louder with each flight.

Finally, my therapist made a suggestion similar to one my ambulance counselor once did: Quit. But this time, I refused, so I was prescribed something in the belief that it would do just enough to take the edge off before my flights. Now mind you, I had never taken drugs before in my life. Aside from the pain-relief medications I had to take for my third-degree burns and multiple surgeries, the strongest thing I had taken was hydrocodone, and not for long. I took my therapist's advice and began taking what he prescribed. It was a drug called clonazepam, and it changed my life for the better. I had always been vehemently against taking any psychotropic drugs. In my alpha-male mind, I believed a real man was supposed to suppress, endure, overcome, and perform his duties with pride. After this, I learned a real man asks for help when he's suffering. Clonazepam did its job. It removed the anxiety and cleared my mind so I could once again focus on flight performance. I was ready to get back in the saddle.

# 13

# Homecoming

By late 2006, I wasn't rich by any means—in fact, I was barely financially stable. Because of my parents I had always been good with money (when I had it), and while I wasn't being paid a ton to be a Rocketman, I didn't have to spend much either. I was on the road most of the time where much of my cost of living was covered, including meals. As a result, I managed to save enough money to put a down payment on a small villa not too far from the hangar in McKinney. Casa de Schlund was not the crazy bachelor pad you might expect to belong to a young jet-pack pilot. I'd wager my neighbors probably thought a retired septuagenarian had bought the place. It was the quietest home on the block.

For much of my adult life up to that point, I'd had very little time for long-term relationships. Yes, I had a few girlfriends, but nothing that got too heavy. The only thing I took seriously was my career. And by late 2006, my career was humming. At times, I was performing almost three weekends a month. And when I wasn't performing, I was thinking about performing. I was constantly working on how I could book more flights. Being a Rocketman wasn't just my job, it had come to define me. So much so that I had actually made the conscious decision that any woman who I let into my life would have to understand that fact explicitly, or there would never, ever be a chance for us to succeed in a relationship. It was at that very time that I was back in Texas in between performances when a certain voice from my past reached out to me.

Shelley Alesso was the gal I had pined for as a young adolescent punk back in my days at Six Flags Magic Mountain. Who inspired me to break games just so I could see her in the arcade when I'd fix them. Who was the only one I called when I scaled the park's legendary tower—and documented it for the whole world to see—all to impress her. We had dated for a bit back in the day, but it had never grown into anything before it fizzled. And yet here she was, reaching out *to me* in email.

Needless to say, I was excited to catch up with Shelley, who was still living in California. After some back-and-forth messaging, I finally had the chance to proudly—no, *arrogantly*—say, "I am a professional Rocketman."

Her response was "Huh?"

But between our emails, she tracked down our Rocketman website and took a look at what I'd been up to. But the site had little information about the nature of life as a Rocketman. I filled in some details as we messaged some more and eventually talked—conversations that went on for hours and hours.

Well, Dan "The Rocketman" Schlund cockily still wanted to show off for Shelley, so he invited her to McKinney for a visit. On the day she arrived, I cleaned up as best I could, put on the nicest clothes I had, and went to meet her at the airport. I got there late, but right as I drove up, she walked out and our eyes met. I had been hoping that she would fall in love with me on the spot, but that's not quite what happened. Instead, I fell in love with her. I even said to myself, *I'm going to marry this girl.*

Much to my astonishment, Shelley's looks hadn't faded in the least. In fact, she looked even more beautiful than I had remembered her. It made me feel insecure. Further, she looked to be not only gainfully employed, but doing quite well. Like the time she went off to college, her success pressured me even more to better myself.

The thing is, Shelley couldn't have cared less whether I was a Rocketman or the guy stocking groceries at the local market. To hear her say it, she "felt led" to contact me after her relationship with Christ deepened. While I was living the Rocketman lifestyle, everyone wanted something or to treat me like a celebrity. But to her, I was just "Dan." And that is exactly what I needed. I wanted someone to care for me *as me*, not because of my alter ego. Or at least a little beyond my alter ego.

For the next week or so, or however long Shelley stayed in Texas, I basically harangued, badgered, and smothered that woman with as much affection, adventure, and conversation as I could. And somewhere along the way, it became clear that our ideals were in line with God, family, and companionship. I couldn't have been happier except for the small fact that she lived in California and I had settled in Texas. But this was just a minor hurdle. And I was, after all, Rocketman, so hurdles meant very little to me.

---

My revived romance with Shelley was a whirlwind affair. We would be engaged on Christmas day of 2006, making that holiday season unimaginably special as that would coincide with being home to see my family and also Kinnie booking me for the biggest flight of my life on New Year's Day 2007. It was going to be at the world-famous Rose Parade, also known as the Tournament of Roses, in Pasadena, where not only tens of thousands of people would line the streets of the city and see the flight, but an estimated four hundred million would be watching worldwide. That was incredibly special and something to be excited about, but I was most excited for the very few people that would be watching me fly for the first time: my family, my friends, and Shelley. Few of my flights were televised locally and all they saw were clips I shared on YouTube (which anyone can still find by searching "Dan Schlund Rocketman"). This was the first time they would see me perform live, right in front of them.

For any performer who does stunt work at the event level, the Rose Parade has to be the top of the pyramid. It is an event that goes all the way back to 1890. The original idea behind the parade was for Californians to showcase the state's beautiful winter weather to the rest of the country. They wanted to show people who had come from the Midwest and the Northeast that they lived in a place where flowers bloomed all year long. After a few years, the parade was such a hit they even added a college football game to the venue. From there, it just got bigger and bigger. For a kid from California who grew up just an hour away from it, being a part of the Rose Parade was like a boy from the Bronx throwing out the first pitch at a Yankees game. I was beside myself. But to raise the stakes even further for me, the Rose Parade officials had elected George Lucas as the parade's Grand Marshal.

Dirty little secret about Pasadena in the wintertime: It's not as warm as you think. Though on the average it reaches the mid-60s Fahrenheit, it is not uncommon at all to dip into the 40s or even lower. And while February is considered a wet month there, rain's been known to come down in January as well. Don't get me wrong, even 60 degrees and wet is balmy compared to much of the rest of the country in the winter, but there would be no guarantee that the weather would be optimal for a Rocketbelt flight. And when New Year's Day 2007 came along, parade-goers were slapped in the face with a downright frigid 44-degree sunrise with the threat of rain. Fortunately, as the day broke, so too did the clouds. And as the crowds swelled around the parade route, the temperature eased into the 60s. Not perfect, but darn close.

I had to strap up early for the flight. Typically, I was never buckled in for more than five minutes before a flight, but the State of Oklahoma had something very special in mind. They had built a float to honor the state's 150th anniversary. And on the float, they had made a small bathroom-sized box where they had me wait in secret. At a designated area, the float would stop, and on a particular spot the box would pop open like a jack-in-the-box and I would be lifted up to the top of the float with a hydraulic lift before blasting off. My task after the blasting off was to fly down the parade route then return and present the Oklahoma state flag to the state's governor, who was riding on the float along with an astronaut, a previous Miss America, and the band The Flaming Lips.

By now I had done hundreds of performances with the Rocketbelt. And since I had been taking my little buddy clonazepam before flights, my nerves had been rock steady. Yet for *this* flight?—my anxiety was off the chart. Let's see: My fiancée was watching me fly for the first time. My family and friends were watching me fly for the first time. And well over one hundred thousand spectators along the parade route were watching, too. And oh, right, the event was being broadcast worldwide, drawing an audience of close to half a billion people. And finally, my childhood idol George Lucas was going to be there too! Well, if there was ever a time to crash and burn . . .

As per custom for a flight of this significance, wives, girlfriends, family, friends and such were not allowed to join the team on-site because it caused unnecessary drama and distraction. But I had rented a toy-hauler motor home so the team and I could arrive together the previous day to avoid the horrendous traffic and prepare. The team and I stayed the night in the RV and woke up early. Shelley, along with my mom and Shannon's wife, stayed in a hotel nearby where they would watch it live. Kinnie was back in Texas enjoying the holidays with his family, but he surely was going to be tuned in; and though not present, in classic Kinnie fashion he was in constant contact with Shannon and the team with regard to every detail of the flight. As of note, the Rose Parade flight was also the debut of the newly rebranded Rocketbelt, the one I own today. Its design was basically the same, save for a complete cosmetic makeover. It was now sleeker, shinier, and was made with a gorgeous Honolulu blue tint. It was stunning.

So, there I was in the box. And between the lid of the box being closed and my flight earplugs, it was pretty close to silent. Still, I could hear and feel the buzz from the crowd outside. And it just kept building. It had been over twenty-five minutes and I was beginning to sweat. I've never been claustrophobic by nature, but it was difficult to be boxed up for so long. I was also beginning to feel numb in my arms and legs from the straps. Remember too that I was carrying about 160 pounds on my back. Even sitting it on the stand was difficult because of the movement. Adrenaline and excitement can only take you so far. But all of that—the anxiety of waiting, the physical wear on my body, the confinement—were the least of my problems. And though I didn't know it at the time, the biggest threat was actually on the Rocketbelt itself. As mentioned, it had been very cold that morning. And per protocol, Kinnie had instructed Shannon and our technician Jeff Ayo to wrap the Rocketbelt's throttle valve in a small towel to keep it from frosting up. Well, unbeknownst to me, that small towel was still on the valve when the support stand was removed for flight.

Ten minutes later, the straps had now completely cut off the circulation in my legs. My shoulder blades had basically gone numb as well. It had been radioed to me that they were waiting for the float to get into the proper position, but I had no idea how long that might be. A minute? *Ten* minutes? If it was any longer, I might have postponed the flight as it was getting to the point where there was no way I could stand. But finally, I felt the float settle and I could hear an announcement broadcast over the parade intercom.

I knew it had to be the moment.

Outside my box, all along the parade route, everyone stopped and turned their attention to the Oklahoma float. At the same time, all watching on television saw cameras doing the same.

It was at this same moment that I received my call.

"Dan, it's go time."

As the top opened up, I was nearly blinded. I had been in the dark for almost forty minutes and the light was as jarring as the moon shifting out of a solar eclipse. It took me a moment to adjust even with my sunglasses on. I was then lifted slowly out of the float where I stood momentarily like a toy soldier and did a quick preflight evaluation. I noticed the float stopped a bit further back than was planned. This meant I had to do a slight right turn to fly around the media tower. That wasn't the best news, as right turns aren't among my most practiced maneuvers. But more concerning for those who knew was that the towel was still on the throttle valve, making it possible to snag the one moving part on the Rocketbelt motor: the throttle valve piston. This is something Kinnie saw immediately on TV and called Shannon to tell him to pause the flight to remove the towel—but Shannon, who noticed Kinnie calling again, must have said to himself, *Why is Kinnie calling me? Doesn't he know we have a flight taking place?* So, he sent Kinnie to voicemail. So worried was Kinnie that he left the room, unable to watch the flight.

Unaware of the towel situation, I focused my concentration on the flight and did what I did, which was turn the throttle. Full blast and instant liftoff!

I have to say, a takeoff had never felt so good. I was just so happy to be off of my feet and let the Rocketbelt do the work now. I elevated, accelerated, and headed for the media tower; I turned right without any issues and then proceeded down the parade route in front of the main stands. It was awesome, entirely controlled. It was like an ocean of people had been parted just for me. I looked down to see the cameras trying to keep up with me as I flew over them. I then tracked my spot and did a tight U-turn—only to find that I flew too far. I needed to get back to the float and to the governor. I checked my timing gauge: fifteen seconds. Plenty of time. I then showed off a bit, accelerating to roughly forty-five mph and climbing a pinch to sixty-five feet in the air. It was a glorious flight. And now it was now time to descend. I checked my timing gauge again: twenty-four seconds—

*Wait a second. Twenty-four seconds?* That meant that the timer was going into the red. In other words, I was now thirty-five feet in the air moving at over forty miles per hour, and I had no idea how much fuel I actually had left. I could drop out of the sky at any second. I immediately proceeded to descend—quickly. Though my timing gauge was in the red, as a seasoned pilot I had a pretty good internal clock and flew it in the red on many occasions. I knew I was going to be cutting it close so I figured, let me just get as low and slow as possible and as close to the mark as I could. Sort of like a plane landing in a cornfield. It would be ugly, but at least I'd be in one piece and save face. As I began to descend, Shannon noticed something I couldn't see: smoke. And it was coming from the small towel that had been wrapped on the valve—very close to the 1,200-degree heat of the motor. It was about to catch on fire. Well, what you don't know can't hurt you. I just kept flying, lower and lower, and as fast as I could. At about twenty feet from the ground, I turned the throttle down and the engine fluttered, and I thought, *Here it comes: Dan Schlund, the human lawn dart.* I braced myself, but the belt still had propellant. I used what it had left and swept in for an *almost* perfect landing.

As soon as I touched the ground, the crowd erupted in cheers. At that same time, Kinnie called Shannon again and this time Shannon answered. Kinnie yelled: "The towel! The towel!"

From nowhere, Shannon came charging toward me and yanked off the smoldering towel. I find it comical that while Kinnie was on the phone and watching the TV in that moment, he could just see Shannon's hand reach into frame and yank the towel off the throttle valve. But no one, not even me, was the wiser. As it would turn out, I had less than a half a second of fuel left in the tank. But the flight was a complete success and now I got to play the part of the hero Rocketman, hamming it up in front of the crowd. As planned, I jogged over to present the Oklahoma state flag to the governor, shook his hand and then did a little victory lap, waving and smiling at the crowd. My next order of business was supposed to be an interview with former Olympic swimmer and gold medalist John Naber for the ABC network, but it was sidetracked just before going on air when one of the parade's cars passed by. It just so happened to be driving the parade's Grand Marshal, George Lucas—*and he waved me over to talk with him!* I ran over to him and shook his hand in front of all the cameras, with his security men trailing me (but what were they going to do, tackle Rocketman?). We had a brief discussion but I was so starstruck and full of adrenaline I couldn't remember anything he said. He may have offered me a role in his next film or had shared with me the key to life. I had no idea. I had just shaken the hand of George Lucas after flying a jet pack in front of nearly half a billion people.

I had a dream job. And I was engaged to my adolescent sweetheart. Life was good. Really, really good.

Now, I only had to figure out how to keep it that way.

# 14

# Running Hot

Prior to marrying Shelley, I had never quite understood the allure of marriage. Most of my male friends were married and I always wondered how we could be out having a great time, drinking a beer or three, when in the middle of it they would abruptly say, "I've got to call it a night and get back to the wifey." And that was it. *Why?* I wondered. It made me think that their wives were back home, sitting next to a sand timer with a sinister look on their faces as the grains slipped away. While others might have needed to get home, I never had any particular reason to return home from a night out or from an event. I liked traveling. I could always hang out an extra day here or there while abroad to see the sights. I took time off to scuba dive the Great Barrier Reef, walk the streets of Paris, sit by the Amazon River and enjoy the distant thunderstorm God presented to me. But Shelley had taught me otherwise. Now that I had her in my life, I *wanted* to go home. Shelley taught me that marriage didn't have to be confining or argumentative. She was supportive of me—and she was also very independent in her own right. She truly was a remarkable woman.

The thing I loved most about my life with Shelley was that it was simple. Quite literally, everything I had ever done in my life was a production. There were tons of moving parts. There was endless maintenance and planning. And there would be repercussions for almost every tiny aspect of what I did. Not with Shelley. She was "plug and play." Easygoing, kind and low-maintenance, she was cool as a Northern California breeze. And the kicker was: She loved me—even with my scar. I didn't even have to do much to maintain her love. Yes, I had certainly tried to impress her in the past and I got a ton of mileage out of climbing that Magic Mountain tower as a kid. But now, unlike the rest of my life, this relationship did not demand stunts. I didn't have to shower her with gifts. I didn't have to take her to fancy places to eat. Heck, I didn't have to do much of anything. I just had to love her. And everything about her made that incredibly easy.

For the next few years, Shelley and I managed to build a good life together. Thankfully, she was able to relocate to Dallas with her job, and we expanded my quiet villa into a beautiful shared home. And though I traveled frequently, I also got to take her with me to several jobs. We went to Paris, traveled to Greece and Turkey. It was a wonderful way to start our lives together. However, I would still struggle in those early years of our marriage as I had trouble confiding in her about my anxiety and insecurity. I still couldn't completely "let myself go" with her because she was so effusively confident and positive. She *believed* in me. Who was I to give her a reason not to?

Another big change after marriage was my event travel. It is a very different dynamic being on the road as a single man than it is being a married one. Not because my behavior would change radically; I was still the outgoing, people-pleasing pilot I had been before marriage. But I also had to be smart. Prior to being married, I was often put in situations that were not conducive to a healthy Christian lifestyle, let alone a married one. There was always a late party to go to where loud music, beautiful women, and loads of alcohol were available in abundance. There were also legions of "hangers-on": shady businessmen who would pitch outrageous schemes to collaborate with them on, offering tons of money and other perks so as to get their hands on the technology of the Rocketbelt. Remember also that the jet-pack industry was totally deregulated. *Anyone* could build a Rocketbelt and market it to the masses. As a younger, single man, I would often be at these parties congregating with a myriad of questionable characters. Why? Because it was fun and I could! Plus, the clients would let the Rocketman take whatever risks he so chose. I was only responsible for myself. But now that I was married, I had to avoid the pitfalls that traveling as a Rocketman had to offer. And I think I did a good job at it.

Marriage would actually end up being very good for my career as a pilot. With no distractions to get into on the road, I put my entire focus into my performances. As a married Rocketman, I also had good role models to aim for in Kinnie and Sheri Gibson, and Shannon and his wife, Missy. Kinnie and Shannon were always totally professional. Being a Rocketman didn't define them like it did me; they were husbands and fathers first. Even the technicians we brought, Jeff Ayo and Sid Goodloe, had strong moral foundations and maintained a Christian character, passing me notes of encouragement, as well as Bible passages and preflight prayers. I needed to do the same, so I began thinking of my work as a service to others, not an identity. It worked. Once I was married, my skills began to elevate and I began to fly with greater precision and grace. Though I would never achieve Eric's level of mastery, I was pretty darn good. In fact, I could even do a few maneuvers he inspired, including a beautiful mid-flight pirouette that had become my signature move.

---

By spring of 2009, Shelley and I had achieved a perfect balance between our work lives and our relationship. We were both doing great at our respective jobs and still very much in love. But there was still something missing. And we both figured out exactly what it was when we got the news that she was pregnant. And I don't think I had ever been more excited. I was going to be *a father.*

At the time, business was going great, but it could've been better. The Rocketman organization had grown well past the point where Kinnie could be picky about the events we booked. However, he also realized that it was in our best interests to keep an aspect of scarcity in our performances. He wanted all of our flights to be special and rare, and to do that, he needed to be selective with our clients and jobs (budget notwithstanding). While this was great for the branding of our business, it wasn't great for me as a Rocketman. I would've flown every day if given the chance—not just because I loved it, but because I was a contracted employee. The more I flew, the more money I made. And with a baby on the way, well, you do the math. For the first time in my adult life, I began to think of life unstrapped to the Rocketbelt. After all, I was in my forties now and you don't become a Rocketman for the gold watch. I had a child on the way and faced a whole new level of responsibility. What if something were to happen to me? Well, as if on cue, something did happen. But it wasn't to me.

It may sound boring, but one of my favorite things to do with Shelley was to sit and watch television with her. We both worked very hard, so it was a nice way to unwind to just sit together and watch stupid shows (of which there were plenty to choose from). We had a particular fondness for *American Idol*, and Shelley loved one of its hosts, Ellen DeGeneres. We had done one other performance on the *Ellen* show in California where Shelley joined me. I was overjoyed when Ellen's talk show reached out to the team and requested a second performance. This was great news that I couldn't wait to share with Shelley. I was hoping she could take a couple of days off and meet me out in Florida, but she couldn't get out of an important work commitment. While I was disappointed, I promised her I would say hi to Ellen on her behalf and get a photo with her.

My flight for Orlando was scheduled to fly out on a Thursday for an early Friday rehearsal followed by the actual show the next day at Universal Studios. But my flight didn't leave until the afternoon, so I was actually at home while Shelley was at work. This was the day of the big meeting she couldn't miss, and she was ready for it. She always looked great for the office, but for her meeting she pulled out all the stops: high-heels and a beautiful blouse. Before I left, I did what I usually do, which was have a quick workout and grab a small bite before packing up. But just as I finished around lunchtime and was about to head to the airport, I received a call from Shelley's office. It was odd for Shelley to call during the day, but I thought maybe she wanted to share how her meeting had gone. But it wasn't Shelley calling.

"Dan, it's Steve," he said. It was Steve McLeod, Shelley's boss.

"I'm sorry if this call is kind of scary," he began, "but we're taking Shelley to the hospital. There's something wrong."

*Sorry not to scare me?* He most certainly did. However, I didn't panic. Instead, I went back to my old EMT experience.

"Steve, don't take her through general admissions, take her to the ER," I said. "And make sure her seat is laid back as far as it can go. I'm on my way."

My first motorcycle, a Honda MR-50, 1974.

The Viper roller coaster at Six Flags Magic Mountain, pre-opening, 1990.

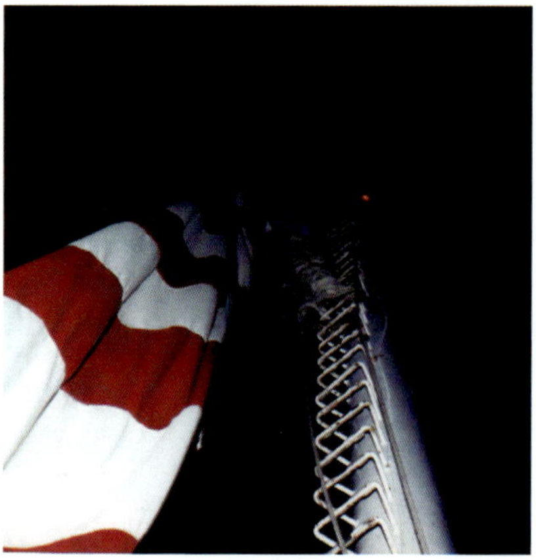

Climbing the iconic
Magic Mountain tower
flagpole in the 1990s.

Me at stunt practice
with Dave Kilde, 1992.

Stunt practice with Dave Kilde (Dave driving), 1992.

When I was ripped and performing stunt work at Six Flags Marine World in Vallejo, California. No CGI—that was an actual fireball behind me.

Playing Lucas Lenard (a character we created out of a compilation of bad guys) at Six Flags Marineworld in Vallejo, California.

Scuba diving in Bali with Sid Goodloe, September 8, 2004.

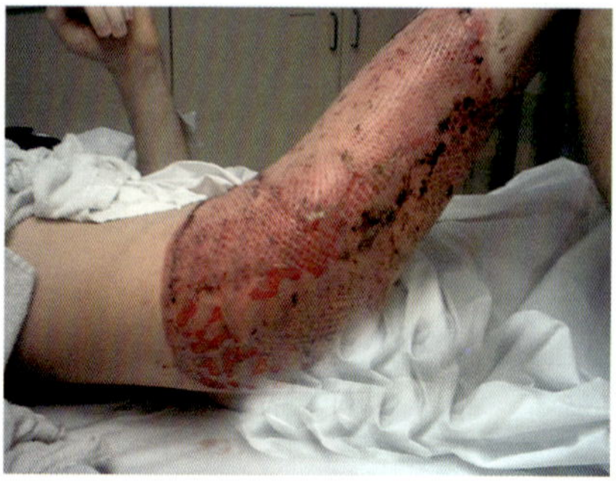

My skin graft surgery. I had lost 185 inches of skin in my accident attempting my third free solo flight with the Rocketbelt.

Meeting George Lucas at the Rose Parade in Pasadena, California, January 1, 2007. George called me over to say hi. It was a high point of my career.

Launching from the Oklahoma float in the 2007 Rose Parade. Six months later I married Shelley just down the street from that spot.

My first jet-pack flight as Boba Fett at the 30th anniversary celebration of *Star Wars* (Celebration IV) held at the Los Angeles Convention Center, May 2007.

Shelley and me on our wedding day, July 21, 2007. What a great memory!

Heisman Trophy pose for the OU–Tulsa game on September 21, 2007.

My Captain Rex (*Star Wars*) flight at the opening ceremonies of Gamescom in Cologne, Germany, October 5, 2009. I launched off a five-story building.

Soaring as Captain Rex at the 2009 Gamescom.

Kinnie and I at the end of the Carnival Parade in Rio de Janeiro, Brazil. I did five flights back-to-back to end up on the elevated platform at the end of the parade.

Me with magic and entertainment duo Penn and Teller on their *Tell A Lie* TV series, October 26, 2011.

ActionFest, Asheville, North Carolina, 2012. My first flight without a helmet.

By the time I reached the ER, Shelley had already been checked in and was waiting to be tested. Steve greeted me as soon as I arrived and shared that Shelley had been very disoriented at work and was incoherent when speaking. I thought maybe it was something simple like low blood sugar or the fact that she was pregnant. But I also feared that it could have been something awful like a stroke.

Staff directed me to the room where Shelley was waiting. As soon as I entered, I nearly burst into tears. I had walked in on hundreds if not thousands of patients during my time as an EMT, but I had never approached anyone that I loved. Shelley looked like a shadow of herself. Her skin was pale and she seemed absolutely despondent. She was also hooked up to all the standard tools of the trade: an IV to keep her hydrated and a monitor for her pulse rate and rhythm. It broke my heart to see, but at least I understood everything on the monitors and they were nominal. I moved to her and cupped her face, but she looked at me as if I were a stranger. And even when she tried to speak, she couldn't enunciate clearly. Though I felt like weeping, I stayed strong and just held her while talking to her. And though she couldn't articulate anything, I got the feeling that she was happy I was there. After about ten minutes, a doctor finally came in and told me they were going to run some tests, including an MRI and blood test, but his preliminary diagnosis was positive. Her heart and pulse were fine, and her pupils weren't dilated. I would then just have to wait for the test results. I immediately called Kinnie and informed him that I would be late to Orlando (if I showed up at all). He told me that they would pray for Shelley and that he would check in when they landed.

It was a strange feeling to be on the other side of a loved one while they were suffering and not be able to do anything about it. My only brush with grievous injury had been after my crash, and I never thought twice about how difficult it was for my loved ones to be on the other side of the gurney, supporting me and praying for me. I kind of took it for granted. Now, here I was, worrying about the health of both my wife *and* my unborn son. I'd been anticipating smooth sailing when it came to the pregnancy even though she was, in her late thirties, a little older than your average first-time parents. And as expected, everything was going as planned until this happened. We'd had the horrible discussion about what we'd do if faced with a choice between Shelley living or the baby. At the time, we chose Shelley. Today, we'd both choose

Danny over either of our own lives; I guess that's the power of parenthood. As I sat in the waiting area feeling the intense anxiety of Shelley's pregnancy scare, I was overcome with gratitude for all of those who had been there for me when I was the one in a hospital bed. I was happy to be able to be there for Shelley for whatever she needed.

We didn't have to wait too long for the good news: There was nothing in the MRI, no stroke, and no viruses. Still, she was admitted for the night for observation. As it turned out, doctors believed that a severe migraine had been triggered by fatigue from her pregnancy. She was then given the drug that I knew all too well, morphine, and it took away the pain while knocking her out for the night. I stayed with her for much of the night until there was really nothing left for me to do but go home.

In what was an absolutely best-case scenario, the next day Shelley was back to her old self. In fact, she even wanted to return to work. But she was told by doctors to rest. She was discharged and sent home. So she was fine. The baby was fine. What can I say but God is good. But the episode had put a good scare into me to be certain, and it added some pressure.

I flew to Orlando. I would soon have *two* mouths to feed.

I arrived in Orlando in a fantastic mood. It is often forgotten how fast life can change—for the good or the bad. And when something comes your way that could have turned out to be tragic, it is a blessing to have that cup passed. That said, I also arrived in Orlando exhausted. I had only gotten about four hours of sleep. Needless to say, you don't want to strap yourself to a Rocketbelt when you aren't fully alert. I could feel my anxiety climbing, a normal response when I'm tired, so I popped a clonazepam, took a deep breath, and headed to the Universal Studios entrance where the team was setting up.

Second only to Disney World, Universal Studios had always been one of my favorite places. While it doesn't sparkle with the "pixie dust" that Disney has, I always found it more accessible. Personable. Disney was about fantasy and immersive experiences. But for me, Universal was about *possibility*. I could never be Peter Pan, but damn if I couldn't try to be one of Marvel's Avengers. When I arrived, Kinnie and the team were already at work, prepping the show.

Also present was a camera crew; Kinnie had recently started hiring them to document our shows. At the time I didn't understand why, as most of what we did, aside from the actual flight, was quite boring. It was just a lot of planning, prepping, and waiting around. But as with many things Kinnie decided to do, documenting our shows was another brilliant move. And none would be more grateful than me when filmmakers ended up using much of the footage for my documentary.

Before I did my test hop for the show, I noticed that Kinnie spent a greater than usual amount of time talking me through a preflight checklist. *Center . . . Check the controls . . . Flap the wings . . . Feet together . . .* I know it probably shouldn't have, but it irked me. In the moment I just found it condescending after all these years of successful flights. Maybe it was because he knew I hadn't slept much or was concerned that I was still worried about Shelley. He might've also had my previous struggles with anxiety on his mind, especially after what I'd recently gone through. I didn't know. It was one of those moments that would have surely had me reeling before I started taking clonazepam. But here, as he continued walking me through what was on its face a very simple flight, that noise that had always been in my head was now silent—the drug was working. And at the end of the day, Kinnie just wanted to do things by the book. So I just listened to him, nodded my head, and focused.

Moments later, I hit the throttle and executed a test hop that would have made Eric blush with envy: just straight up and smooth like one of the rockets launching out of Cape Canaveral. I then flew forward with a controlled acceleration before gaining a little altitude—just because. Then I turned around and came back. We were now ready to see Ellen and her producers.

Like the first professional flight I had ever done, the one for P. Diddy in Miami, this performance too would incorporate me as a look-alike. The flight itself was pretty simple, be it a tad far in distance in terms of my landing target, about two hundred yards over water and landing on a tight but long stretch of stage. At this point of my career, it was a piece of cake. The toughest aspect of the job wasn't going to be the flight, it was going to be what I would wear for the flight—or more accurately, what *Ellen* would choose to wear. And at the time, Ellen had not chosen her wardrobe, still deciding between five outfits. My only real concern when doing body-double flights was making sure I had a suitable helmet. It was a sign of good producers that everything on set was cheap, so naturally, the helmets they had purchased looked like they came from a costume shop. Typically, I would never complain to a client about what I would wear or how I would fly, but I always drew the line at helmets. They would have to do better or I wasn't going to go up.

Since Ellen hadn't picked out her outfit yet, I decided to do the rehearsal flight in my jeans and sneakers. In all honesty, it was my favorite way to fly. Just put on the belt and go for it. For the show flight, I would lift off behind the giant Universal Studios globe, move forward slowly until I reached an altitude equal to the "Universal" wording on the globe, then drop the handles and kick it into high gear. It was a "hot" flight—that is, I instantly popped off the ground and began to climb at an intense rate, something that I absolutely *loved*. Maybe it was the propellant or weather conditions, but the Rocketbelt is like that sometimes. Sometimes it just runs hot. I pulled back on the handles to slow down and began to make my turn but overestimated the speed, wind, and distance and ended up whizzing past my mark. I then increased my altitude as I flew over the top of the stage. As I did, I looked down at my timer: sixteen seconds. Plenty of time. There was a brief moment of suspense on the stage below as I made a smooth turn and lined up for my landing approach. I then gave another cursory glance to my timer: sixteen seconds. . . . *What?!* My timer had stopped. This had been a situation that happened once or twice in the past during training, and we thought we'd fixed it. But now I was well over sixty feet in the air and had no idea how much time I had left in the tank. I could have fallen out of the sky at any moment. I had to think quick. I made a swift but controlled descent. I wasn't very close to my landing spot, but I also wasn't worried about it. What concerned me was running out of fuel and doing a face-plant into the pavement below. But I kept my cool, dropping as low and fast as I could until . . .

I made a beautiful landing. It may have been off the mark, but I didn't care. I then punctuated it with an Ellen-style dance as I moved backstage.

I am not often satisfied with rehearsal flights, but as footage would prove, the practice flight for the Ellen show was one of the best we had ever done. I was at the perfect elevation and the perfect speed. All my maneuvers were silky smooth. And even my dancing wasn't bad. The producers were blown away, as were all those bystanders who got to see it. And even the team and I were high-fiving all over the place. It was just one of those times where everything went right.

But apparently, they hadn't gone right enough. While we were yukking it up, excited to do the real thing, Ellen had reached out to the producers and canceled. We weren't given a reason either. They just said that Ellen simply wanted to do something else for the show. The producers seemed upset at the situation, and I'm sure there was more to the story than they shared. But that was it. There was no other flight. No funny dance from Dan. And no photo with Ellen for Shelley. At least we still got paid.

Technically, the Orlando trip had been a disaster. At the end of the day, we didn't finish the job. However, I saw the trip as an incredible step forward in my skills as a pilot as well as my demeanor under pressure. I kept my cool after I overshot my mark on a flight, and even with my timer mishap I still managed a stellar landing. Even after the client had canceled, I kept my composure. In the past, any of this would have roiled me. I would've blamed myself and obsessed over something that I said or did that would have made Ellen cancel. But this time, I didn't. I was cool under pressure from the moment I arrived in Orlando. Besides, what do I care if it was on TV? I got to fly around the globe at Universal and down the waterway. I was able to look back and recognize how much I'd grown as a performer, and I enjoyed it. No ride in Orlando could compete with what I did!

But the thing about all of this lack of anxiety is that I didn't attribute any of it to myself. I didn't attribute my improved skills and professionalism to the maturity that came with marriage and a change in lifestyle. Instead, I attributed it to a little secret that I kept to myself: my little friend, clonazepam.

Though my taking clonazepam before flights was no real "secret" (even Kimmie was known to take it at times), I had never made it known that I'd begun taking the drug more frequently. After all, if it had worked so well for me before a flight, why not take it on practice days too? And if they worked on practice days, why not on my off days? And if a half a milligram was good, wouldn't one milligram be better? Soon enough, I was popping them daily, anytime I felt anxiety, which was becoming more common. In retrospect, I never felt like I physically needed the drug, I just enjoyed being anxiety-free. If I skipped a few days or forgot to take one, I never freaked out or broke into a panic attack. But the danger for me was that I thought I *needed* to take it. Yes, the drug calmed me, but it also had a placebo effect for me. It became my security blanket. It had entered into my psyche and became my invisible sidekick. But the other side effect that clonazepam produced in me was a manic work ethic. I know that is not typically associated with the drug as it is classified as a benzodiazepine, which is a central nervous system depressant. But by removing my anxiety, clonazepam freed me to dive fully into my job. And while taking it did come with feelings of tranquility, the rush of the adrenaline also made me ebulliently confident. I was often so " drunk" with endorphins after performances or practice that it took me hours or even days to come down. But soon after, the anxiety would slowly creep back into my life; the clonazepam was losing its potency. Well, not a problem. Clonazepam is after all a fairly lightweight benzodiazepine. So I got prescribed something more potent to take before flights—Xanax.

# 15

# Rocket Dad

On October 1, 2010, Shelley gave birth to our son, Danny. It wasn't a surprise to me that we had a boy. Whether it was a message from God or a premonition or both, I had just always known that my first child would be a son. I also knew he would be blond and blue-eyed and share my name. All of this came true with the birth of Danny. However, it was a surprise *when* he came into this world.

Daniel Lawrence Schlund was scheduled to be born on September 28th. Naturally, we planned around it, and a few days before—on the very day Shelley's sister Amy arrived from California for the birth—Shelley started having contractions. It was the first time I told Kinnie I was not available for any flights. I didn't care how much it paid or where it was. I was officially "out of service." As an EMT who had seen plenty, I wasn't the typical first-time father. I knew that contractions didn't mean that Shelley would go into labor immediately. We had time. So, we calmly gathered everything we needed for the hospital. After several hours without further contractions, it became pretty clear that Shelley wasn't going to give birth just yet. We stayed home.

A few hours later, Shelley still showed no signs of going into labor. Our doctor thought we should schedule an "induced delivery." But Shelley and I both agreed to let nature take its course. With now over nine months of pregnancy and still no baby, however, even Shelley was getting antsy. So we did what any nine months' pregnant woman would want to do. We went to the Texas State Fair and walked around for hours—and it worked. The next night, September 30th, those contractions returned in force. Shelley had been hungry and we knew they wouldn't feed her at the hospital, so I stopped along the way to pick up some Subway before speeding her there. We checked in and waited. And waited. And finally, at around 3:30 a.m. on October 1, 2010, Danny came into the world. The best part was that since I was an EMT, the doctor let me gown up and deliver my own son. (Years later I would have the privilege of baptizing him too.)

I was overjoyed to share the news of Danny's arrival with everyone. Obviously, family would be notified immediately, but I didn't want to tell everyone else at the same time like in a post on Facebook. I wanted to call people and share the good news. Naturally, one of my first calls was to Kinnie, and while he was kind and said all the right things, I got the sense that there was something wrong. He just wasn't his usual, positive self. I didn't say anything and didn't really think twice about it until not long after when I heard from his wife, Sheri. She too seemed a bit down. And after talking for a bit, she finally shared why: Kinnie had been struggling with anxiety and depression. She didn't go into great detail about it, but after she hung up, a wave of concern washed over me. I loved Kinnie. He was the rock of our organization. But it just reminded me that *nothing* in this life lasts. That goes for good times. Success. And even health. It made me all the more appreciative for what I had—and especially my newborn son, Danny.

---

Fatherhood would change me in an even more profound way than marriage had. Marrying Shelley changed my heart. And it made me change my habits, my work ethic, and the way I communicated. But when Danny came into the world it changed *my soul.* It's one thing to share a life as I was with Shelley. And it's a beautiful gift from God. But it is another thing to *produce* a life.

To *shape* a life. To be totally *responsible for* a life. Of course, all of that is super scary too. That's what makes fatherhood (and motherhood) so special.

One thing that I didn't fully understand would happen when I became a father was that once Danny came into the world, I couldn't imagine my life without him. It made it hard to remember my past. I never thought I was capable of loving anyone the way I loved him. From the moment I first held him, I was overcome with a feeling of intense determination to do anything I could to make his life fantastic. And as I did, I thought of my own father and how he probably had the same feeling when holding me for the first time.

For the first couple of years after Danny's birth, things were going quite well with the Rocketman organization despite Kinnie's struggles and Eric's decision to step away. He had been a Rocketman for much longer than I, and being well into his late forties by now, he wanted to try something new. We were also all very excited for a side project Kinnie had come up with that would be lucrative for all of us. This was especially important to me because now that I had a family, I really had to step up my game financially. Shelley was taking time away from her career to raise little Dan, and my salary as Rocketman just wasn't cutting it. I needed to make more money. As mentioned, Kinnie had been hiring camera crews at all of our events to document the performances. I had thought that maybe the reason he was doing this was for his family or just posterity's sake; we'd never really talked about it. But he had shared some footage with some people he knew in the television industry and they were blown away, convinced that a reality series could be centered around the Rocketman business. We were all incredibly excited about the prospect and our spirits were all imbued with a new level of energy. But I had even bigger plans. I thought I could use the show as a springboard for my own name and branch out into public speaking, writing inspirational books and making special appearances. I stepped my game up even more as Rocketman with one goal in mind: I wanted to be the *best*.

As the prospect of selling our show to a network grew closer, another huge blessing came our way when we were booked for one of the biggest performances we had ever done. Though it would be far from the most prestigious, it would be among the most lucrative. It was for the Africa Cup of Nations (held in Angola), which is like the World Cup for the continent of Africa. Tournament officials wanted to do something unique and special for the trophy ceremony at the end of the games and had requested two pilots. And since Eric wasn't available, that meant Kinnie himself would have to dust up on his skills and go up with me.

It had been more than ten years since Kinnie had flown, and though nobody would say anything, his anxiety was palpable. Personally, I admired him a great deal for getting back on the horse, and I think he embraced the opportunity as a "last hurrah." There was the small problem in the fact that he had never actually flown any of the new belts he had built. But Kinnie was a Rocketman. And we were all very much reminded of this as he hummed through his retraining on the wire and did remarkably well off of it. In a great role reversal, it was now me watching and advising him on his flights. But I admittedly didn't have much to offer.

---

Angola was an interesting place. It was almost so stereotypically "African" that it looked like a movie set. It was hot, dry, and teeming with people. In the town where we stayed, women carried goods on their heads and shopkeepers touted their wares in carts. We stayed in a "four-star" hotel that looked like something that would charge by the hour back in the States. In fact, the hotel would run out of water on occasion, and we couldn't even take a shower. With no internet or TV, options for entertainment were limited. But that doesn't mean we didn't have a good time. We had met another group that were also performing at the Cup. They had a massive production that included a cast of Cirque du Soleil–type performers who used cables to shoot the cast members fifty feet in the air for an aerial dance. Not only did their production team strap Kinnie and me into their cables for a little demonstration, but later we drove around the countryside with their crew and saw some of the sights and met people in their villages. The people were incredibly friendly and kind but they lived in staggering poverty. It certainly made me grateful for the comforts I had back home.

---

While meeting new people and having fun had been a staple in my Rocketman travel throughout the early part of my career, I was now at the point where I could have done without it. Every trip was a business trip, and to that end I treated it as such. So when the practice flights for the Cup came along, there was no downtime. We went to work immediately. For this particular performance, which was a first of its kind for any of us, Kinnie and I were to take off at the same time from opposite sides of the field and approach each other in the sky; we would then loop around one another before coupling up and landing together. I would be the pilot carrying the Cup's gold-plated globe-topped trophy, but we would present it together to the official of the tournament.

Though the flight itself was a simple one, it was both strange and exhilarating to see another Rocketman in the sky with me. But not just a "Rocketman." It was *Kinnie Gibson.* Kinnie wasn't just my friend and mentor, he was a legend. And as I look back on this memory, it was the absolute high point of my time with him as a fellow Rocketman. Unfortunately, the low point was just hours away.

Early that evening, I was in my room winding down for the night when a knock on my door preceded an envelope with my name on it being slipped underneath. I picked it up, opened it, and pulled out a generic agreement with the heading "Talent Release." I didn't know what it was for, and as I stood there reading it over, there was another knock on my door. I opened it to see Shannon holding the same thing with a confused look on his face.

"It's for the TV show Kinnie is making," he said.

Not only hadn't we heard anything about this before, but the contract was for a "full release of our likeness and rights to our images being used in perpetuity." In other words, if we signed it, they could use our images, performances, and likenesses at will without payment. We both walked over to Kinnie's room to ask for an explanation. Kinnie wasn't there, but his son West answered the door. We asked him about the releases and he downplayed it, saying it was just a formality the network needed before we engaged in negotiations for the future TV show. I didn't blame the kid, but Shannon and I explained that we weren't going to sign any such agreement, because we knew it would be detrimental to negotiating a rate once the show was sold. So that was that.

About a half hour later, I got another knock on my door. This one much harder. It was Kinnie, and he was enraged.

"What the hell is your problem, you ungrateful shit?!" he began.

He then just laid into me. Kinnie had never yelled at me before, ever. I don't know if it was the stress of flying or his anxiety medication or something else altogether, but I was actually in shock. So, I let him unload until he was finished, which seemed like a good five minutes. But after he was done, I still stood my ground. I wasn't going to sign the document, and it was unprofessional to make such a request of us at that time and place.

"Kinnie," I said. "This document waives all my rights in perpetuity."

"No, it doesn't!" he insisted. "You own ten percent of Powerhouse Productions."

I disagreed. "Kinnie, signing this document would be a detriment to me, my family, and newborn son. You have to understand that."

He didn't. And for a brief moment, as he was gnashing his teeth, I thought he was going to punch me. But he then just suddenly turned and, without saying a word, walked out.

I wasn't going to spend all these years flying and almost dying to sign away all my rights with only a "hope" that he would be fair. These negotiations take attorneys and multiple contract variations to iron out.

After the blowup, I was so angry that I considered leaving, going so far as to make some calls about the quickest flights out of Angola. But I needed the money and I had made a commitment to do the flight. That commitment ultimately overruled any initial anger. Thinking back on my live stunt-show days, I reminded myself of the verbal agreement I made with Kinnie years ago. "We will have disagreements, but the show must go on."

Needless to say, the show did go on, but it was not our best performance. Not because of the tension between us, but because our timing was off. Kinnie's coordinator signaled him to fly before mine did, and I wasn't ready. I scrambled to put on my helmet and then remove the safety lock on the throttle, and then took off. Unfortunately, we didn't fly in unison like in the practice flight. As I saw it, it was a disaster—just two jet-pack pilots flying around aimlessly. Considering how mad we both were and the fact that we hadn't even spoken before the flight, I'm surprised we didn't crash into one another mid-flight. But we did finish the job. The crowd applauded, though I don't really know why. Before we left for home, Kinnie apologized, but I didn't feel it was fully sincere. And that was it.

Then it got worse.

Back home, days later when it was time to get paid, I was given my percentage of the job but only paid on half of the contracted amount. My percentage should have been a percentage on the full amount, which had always been our agreement and standard practice; but Kinnie told me since he did half the flight, I only got a percentage on one half of the fee. So in effect, he basically deducted tens of thousands of dollars off my paycheck. I was incensed. I worked for years making less than minimum wage, when you calculated it all out. The Angola show had been an opportunity to reap the benefits of all my hard work—it would have been my biggest payday ever—and it didn't happen. I was screwed! Was this because I didn't sign the talent release? Probably. This was an exceptionally bad blow for me. Not only was the money from that event intended to go a long way toward the nest egg I had been trying to build for Shelley and Danny, but it was also going to give me the oxygen I needed to figure out what the next steps of my life might look like.

And because I'd been so grateful for the anticipated payday, I had also been planning on doing something special with some of the money as a way of "tithing" to God, who had been so good to me. I had once promised an orphanage in India that when I could, I would donate enough money to purchase a bus for the kids. When I booked the Angola job, I called the director there and shared the good news. They were so excited. But after being denied half of those expected funds, I had to call him and back out of my pledge unceremoniously.

It was demoralizing, and I knew this was the beginning of the end. I had dedicated my entire career to working with Kinnie. I'd been loyal. I'd been a hard worker. I had almost died on two occasions working for him. If money was going to take precedent over my sacrifices, perhaps it was time to move on. And now I began to consider starting my life over again with nothing.

# PART FOUR

# CRASH

This is what the Lord says: You know if a man falls down,
he gets up again. And if a man goes the wrong way,
he turns around and comes back.
—Jeremiah 8:4

# 16

# Рокетмен (Rocketman)

After my blowout with Kinnie in Angola, I had to do some soul-searching to figure out what God wanted for me. The problem was, I still wanted to fly and I couldn't entertain anything else until I exhausted all of my opportunities. I began by reaching out to Kinnie in attempt to amend our contract, offering that I would market and book my own flights if he would allow me to "rent" the Rocketbelt from him. Kinnie refused. If I wanted to fly, he told me, it would be under our original contract. Full stop.

At one point in time, I was so exhausted, frustrated, and demoralized that I told Kinnie I was not going to fly anymore. The stress was too much. Shortly after that I received a letter from his attorney. He threatened me: If I didn't fly, he would sue. But I had a card up my sleeve. The contract states I have to fly only if I feel "safe" doing so. Well, I didn't feel "safe" anymore.

After that showdown, cooler minds prevailed. Kinnie said with true honesty: "I know I can't make you fly but I want to try and work this out with you." I offered to just buy one of the Rocketbelts, but the price was too outrageous. We went back and forth on a number of other propositions, but none were suitable for either of us. We even went to mediation at our church to settle the issues with the old contract, but in the end, I gave up my 10 percent ownership in the company and dismissed the Angola money in return for nullifying the current contract.

Although the old contract was null and void, we continued to work together under the same stipulations, such as my percentage and shared responsibilities. And although it was a step backwards for me, the settlement wiped the slate clean for future negotiations on the anticipated TV show. Despite it all, it was important for both Kinnie and me to find a way to continue working together. During this time, Kinnie was working on producing the TV show around the Rocketman family, and we filmed a number of episodes in places like New Zealand for their Big Day Out music festival, and in Rio de Janeiro for the Carnival parade. Kinnie had no idea where this might take the company and didn't want to enter a new agreement with me. I wanted to be sure I had a stake in the TV show and not be replaced or discarded just when things were taking off. Behind closed doors they discussed bringing in a new pilot, possibly Kinnie's son West or his friend Trevor Habberstad, a young and upcoming stuntman. I knew that meant I would be replaced before the show even got going. Had I signed that "generic agreement" in Angola, they could've used my footage and not owed me a dime. I knew I'd been right in insisting on protecting myself. With another pilot, I'd have no bargaining power. With my growing resentment, I was now becoming more of a liability than an asset in Kinnie's eyes.

Slowly, I began to see signs of my replacement. Managing the Rocketman Facebook page was taken away from me and given to West. My name and picture was removed from the website and was replaced with mostly Kinnie's family photos with job titles and such: "The new Rocketman crew." I was in a very precarious position. I had worked so hard for so little money for so many years, risking my life in the process, because I loved the work—but also because I had a plan to eventually reap more substantial financial rewards from it by transferring the experience into a speaking career. It was a ten-year investment in myself. Something I could eventually make some real money with without risking my life. Unfortunately, it was a race between getting the TV show produced and how much stress and anxiety I could endure given my newly tenuous position with Kinnie. And the anxiety was winning. Did I have enough endurance over my anxiety to make it to the finish line? It felt like a losing battle. All I needed was to make a name for myself. Then, after the first season, they could hire whoever to take my place and my speaking career could take over. Until then, I had to keep flying, making appearances and putting on a good show. Still, I did the best job I could with every performance.

The pursuit of the TV show was taking years of development, and everyone wanted a fair piece of the pie. But with no control, the team and I were at Kinnie's mercy. This added to my anxiety and animosity. Kinnie, for his part, was doing his best to bring the show to fruition and simply couldn't answer the increasing questions the team and I had. He simply didn't have answers to them. It was too early for promises.

The dream of a TV show gave us all the encouragement to carry on, but in truth it felt like there was a carrot being held in front of the horse and I was the horse's ass.

All of this drama made life difficult for me, and in all likelihood, I'm sure it made the lives of others close to me difficult too. I had always been industrious and enthusiastic when it came to my jobs. I always went above and beyond the scope of my work because not only did I think it was the right thing to do, I had always loved what I'd done. But after everything that happened with Kinnie, being a Rocketman just felt like work. However, as my days there wound down, I still reminded myself that even a bad day as Rocketman was still a pretty darn good one. Such was the case when we booked a performance in Russia in 2011.

---

Russia has meant very different things at different times to us in the United States. As the dominant power of the former Soviet Union, it was a mysterious and forbidden place. In fact, up until the latter part of the twentieth century, which represented most of my lifetime, American citizens were not allowed to travel behind the Iron Curtain. Because of this, I had always had a great curiosity about Russia, and when Kinnie reached out with the opportunity, I was genuinely excited. And though it didn't mean that we were "at peace," a trip together to the former Soviet Union would go a long way to reconciliation.

The events leading up to our flight in Red Square do warrant mentioning. First off, before we even took the job, there were several hiccups. As it is well known, Russia is not the warmest place in the world. And even during late spring or early fall there can be very frigid days, but they had wanted us in the dead of winter. Kinnie would not take the chance. We would fly only when the fuel and belt were warm enough to fly. We also had to negotiate how the belts and fuel would be transported, which in itself came with a myriad of problems with only expensive solutions. Doing business with Russia is every bit the headache you can imagine. If you think going to your local Department of Motor Vehicles to renew a driver's license is a pain in the ass, try applying for work permits and shipping manifestos for bringing corrosive chemicals into Moscow. But the biggest hurdle we had to overcome with booking the Russian flight was the fact that when it came down to it, our Russian client simply couldn't believe that we could really fly. They truly thought it could have been a hoax and that no such Rocketbelts existed. And it didn't matter that we had thousands of pictures and hundreds of videos of flights to prove we could. They didn't believe it. Finally, after months of haggling, the Russian client agreed to the contract and put up the down payment. But it even came with a warning: *You guys better be able to do what you say you can!*

---

The first word that comes to mind when thinking about my trip to Russia is "surreal." We've all seen the Kremlin on the news. We've seen Moscow and St. Petersburg. We've seen men in their round, fur-covered *ushanka* hats and women in their babushka kerchiefs wrapped around their heads. But to be there and see it and walk among the people was absolutely mind-bending for me. Because it was one of those situations where my expectations and imagination matched exactly what was reality. One of the things that I discovered while traveling is that I needed to throw out any of my misconceptions about a country or people before I visited. For instance, Abu Dhabi was like Beverly Hills on steroids. It was the nicest and most modern place in the world. I thought Nicaragua would be poor and miserable—and yes, its people were certainly poor, but they were also wonderful and filled with joy. I had also imagined Russia would be a beautiful place, but also a cold place with cold people, a place where it would be very difficult to do what we needed to do because of the layers of government bureaucracy that would impede us. And guess what? That's exactly the way it was! (That is, until we scratched the surface a bit.)

We arrived in Moscow in the evening where a non-English-speaking taxi driver had been sent to pick us up. The first thing that struck me about the place was the traffic. It was awful. Not just L.A. awful but miles-of-stop-and-go awful. There was actually a sign on someone's back window that said in big English letters: Fuck Russian Roads. We were on a highway that seemed more like a parking lot and we must have only moved about fifteen feet in our first hour. Hours later, as we inched toward our exit, I was convinced that it would only be a prelude of what to expect. Once we were eventually off the highway, even though it was dark, at least I could finally look around. I was stunned. But not in a grand way. It seemed to be an endless landscape of super-large apartment complexes, three football fields wide and at least fifty stories high. And they went on and on. Some of the buildings were lit and alive. Others, completely dark. They looked like some of the apartment projects you find in inner cities across the U.S., only they were ten times the size, like little cities unto themselves.

I was surprised when we arrived at our hotel because it blended in with everything else. It was generic. Gray. Huge. Like a dormitory. And while the people there were polite and professional, more than anything they were *perfunctory*. It was as if everything had to be done in accordance to a playbook. There was no room for improvisation or small talk. I had thought that we would be treated like rock stars as we had been when we visited so many other countries. I had envisioned myself holding court at a local bar, throwing down shots of Russian vodka while sharing stories to a group of locals who were just enthralled with the "crazy American" who flew a Rocketbelt. Well, this vision went out the window pretty fast. As soon as I checked into my drab room, I cleaned up, called Shelley to wish her and Danny a good-night, and went to bed.

---

There are no two Rocketbelt performances that are exactly alike. The flight pattern can be the same. The movements can be the same. But wind, weather, time of day, they all play a part. So too does locale. And there was something about flying in Red Square, which had represented the very epicenter of the former Soviet Union at the height of the cold war, that made this flight even more different than any flight I, or anyone, had ever done. I don't mean to overstate its importance. By 2011, Red Square had practically turned into the site of the Blarney Stone in Ireland; the place was teeming with tourists. To represent an American company that was utilizing cutting-edge technology for self-propelled aviation to fly over Russian airspace in a device created by the U.S. Army to someday fight the communists—that was a truly amazing experience from both a historical and personal perspective. It was also an epic moment for Kinnie, who was there with me to manage the flight.

It had been less than a year since our mediation. Being the first performance Kinnie and I worked on together, I was a little nervous about residual effects from our business disagreements affecting the flight; but those worries quickly subsided once we got to work. Both Kinnie and I, at the end of the day, were professionals, and we actually got along surprisingly well. He and I were our old selves; previous animosity notwithstanding, we enjoyed each other's company. We were Rocketmen. And this is exactly what I was thinking as I was standing there, right in front of Lenin's grave, thinking about making Rocketman history.

And standing some more. And waiting some more.

Several hours later, I was still standing and waiting. And getting cold. Our client had pitched a nice tent on an elevated wood platform with plenty of heaters. Our equipment was there and we were ready to go. All we needed was permission. But it just hadn't come. As a matter of record, as required by Russian authorities, both Kinnie and I had to secure official "Rocketman licenses"—but they had been fake. There was no such thing as a Rocketman license, and yet it was still required by the government. We told this to our client and their reply was simply, "Well, make them." And so we did. I thought that maybe these fake licenses were being scrutinized, and I had the briefest thought that a car would speed into the square and skid to a stop right in front of us. I then pictured a pair of surly KGB agents pouring out of it to arrest Kinnie and me on the spot. But to be honest, if anyone could grant a license to fly a Rocketbelt it was us, so in a sense, they *were* legal. The issue was that just days before we arrived, Russia had been the site of a terrorist attack in in St. Petersburg, wherein a train had been bombed. Twenty-six people had been killed and many more injured, so the country was on high alert. As a result, our client had been trying to push the flight through, but it was being delayed at every level by very high-up officials. After we passed more hours waiting, the test flight was postponed and we were told to return the following day.

The client picked us up the next morning at eight thirty for what we thought would be an eleven o'clock test flight followed by a rehearsal at one in the afternoon. But when we arrived at Red Square, we discovered that the power had gone out in the tent. That meant that the fuel we had kept warm would now have to be reheated. But the test hop being delayed and cold fuel was the least of our problems. We still didn't have permission to go *up*. Again, we waited. All day. And again, nothing. Finally, at the very end of the day, at a time when we might have salvaged at least getting in a test hop, the word from Russian officials came in. It was a resounding "*Nyet!*" The reason we were given was that Russia could not provide us any certificates for flying Rocketbelts. Well, *of course!* No country does. Not even the U.S. We wanted to scream.

Our client soon revealed to us, however, that the *real* reason we weren't allowed to go up was that no one wanted to take responsibility for our flight, especially after the recent terrorist bombing—no way were they going to risk another disastrous event—not to mention the fact that both Vladimir Putin and President Dmitry Medvedev would be there in person. I pleaded for them to let me do a test flight to show it was safe—secretly, I wanted to say I flew in Red Square—but the answer was still . . . *Nyet!* So we packed up the equipment and took off. I was very disappointed. That is, until our client came up with a Plan B.

Our client represented one of the largest media companies in Russia—and they had an idea. Since they were responsible for the entire fee whether we flew or not, why not let us fly *privately*? So, they decided to take us to the one place where the government didn't have a say: the roof of their headquarters, another gargantuan building. And this is where the real "Russia adventure" began.

First off, night had fallen and it was getting cold. Secondly, neither Kinnie nor I or any of our crew had any idea where these "headquarters" could be. They could've been in Siberia for all we knew. But at that point, we were in Russia, and we just wanted to fly. I suppose we might have agreed with anything.

We drove for what seemed like hours, and when we finally reached our clients' headquarters, I had no idea where we were. In fact, I still don't. But the building itself looked like a mountain. It must have been fifty stories high and at least a block wide. Oddly, though, the roof on top of it looked like a patch of land plucked from McKinney, Texas. It was actually made up of dirt, sod, and stone. It also provided one of the most beautiful views I had ever seen. I had been around the world and seen some spectacular sites, but I can tell you with conviction, the Russian countryside at sunset was breathtaking. It was a sprawling vista of mountains and lakes and gorgeous rural farms. I was impressed. I was also further impressed by our clients. Suddenly, they weren't the stodgy business people we had been dealing with. Now with no looming government officials or restrictions to deal with, they let their guard down and were warm, funny, and open.

It was on top of that roof the next morning at four a.m., warming myself in a small tent among the small cement cliffs, a beautiful lake view, and the frigid Russian wind, that I would take flight into Russian airspace. Of course, we had to set up and do a test hop first, but working with their crew, it couldn't have gone smoother. The director wanted a very precise flight. I was to lift off the summit with good power, hit my altitude, then accelerate to their designated mark before landing with their iconic tower in the background. Oh, but there was a caveat. I was to do this wearing a Santa Claus costume. I don't know exactly why. Perhaps it was for a promotion for the network, or maybe it was just footage that they wanted to get. But that's what they asked for, so that's what I wore.

The Russian flight may have been a high point for me as far as my technical skill with the Rocketbelt. To be honest, my precision on the flight was even surprising to me. I flew quickly, nailing my marks and managing perfectly straight lines of flight. However, I didn't quite stick the landing. As I was making my final approach, I found myself running short on time, so I made a quick left turn. And whether it was the cold, or simply that I used more throttle than normal, I ran out of fuel just as I was coming down. I fell to the ground hard, first to my legs, then to my knees and forward. With my arms I was able to save the handles from damage, but it came at an expense of great physical pain. Still, I popped up immediately. I was an American. And Americans didn't show weakness—especially in front of Russians. But after a few pats on the back and some smiles, you can bet that later I wailed like an infant who needed milk.

---

Though the Russian trip was a great experience and it was good to reconnect with Kinnie, after I returned home I realized that I could no longer continue with that life. I had bills to pay, and with no other options, I needed to do something else. Shelley stood by my side and was open to whatever I wanted to do. She was, of course, concerned over finances, but she could see the rising anger in me and felt helpless in providing direction. After all, Shelley was a corporate woman, and what I did was completely different. After much thought and prayer, I decided to shift gears and attempt to get into the corporate world myself. But despite all my international experience in so many fields, I couldn't translate it into a bona fide résumé, let alone a job offer. Then it occurred to me. I loved working on the ambulance, and to add to that, I would have the knowledge to protect my family in a medical emergency. I decided to go back to school and become a paramedic. My thoughts were that I could work as a paramedic and just fly the belt on the side. This way I would have a steady income but still make some extra money while continuing to do something that I loved until the TV show was ready. I ensured Kinnie that I would still be a full-time Rocketman. Since we only flew once or twice a month now, I could balance both my paramedic and Rocketman duties.

I enrolled in an expedited nine-month program at Emergency Medical Training Services in Dallas, Texas, and without having any idea of how I would pay for the tuition. But as He had done for me throughout my life, God had a way to provide. And no sooner did I enroll when I received a call from my old stunt friend, Dave Kilde. Well, after we caught up a bit, he mentioned that he and a stunt-coordinator friend named Hunter Brown had been hired to produce a stunt show for the 2012 World's Fair in Yeosu, South Korea. This is the same Hunter Brown that coordinated the low-budget film Dave and I worked on so many years ago and who was the coordinator before me in Taiwan for that other company who tried to intimidate me. For the fair, they were going to feature a water jet pack, and they asked if I'd like to produce that portion of the show because of my Rocketman reputation. We struck a deal, and it was then that I created T-Minus Productions, which would be the corporation for anything jet-pack related. I then managed the show from afar while attending paramedic school, both of which went great—and I was able to pay for my school at EMTS.

---

Returning to school was intimidating. Not because I wasn't bright enough or wasn't excited to begin, but because I had gotten older. The last time I had been in school I was in my early twenties. At that time, I was a spunky kid, full of life and dreams and possibilities. Now, in my forties, I was a man with a wife and child and many scars trying to figure out a way to hang on. But even though I was very much different than that kid who had trained to be an EMT, I was still the resilient man my mother and father had raised. So when the rubber hit the road with my studies, I tackled the opportunity like a champion, studying hard and doing my work, and I would end up graduating in the top third of my class. And unlike high school, I really enjoyed it. Not bad for an old man.

On December 6, 2012, I was certified as a paramedic. I was also a volunteer firefighter for the small town of Celina, Texas, and even got a job with CareFlite in Dallas. I was stationed in Ferris, Texas, running 911 calls in that area. For the most part it was pretty boring since not much happened in Ferris. So I worked there for a short while, until I got an idea. I noticed there had been a big increase in television and film production in and around Dallas, and I figured I had made good money as a set medic in Los Angeles. I thought, why not do the same thing here as a paramedic? So in my downtime at the station I started reaching out to various producers, production heads, and events organizers and offered them my services. A few months later, my work was rewarded with my first set medic gig. It was for a low budget commercial that wasn't the greatest of gigs, but with that job and a $500 investment, my company National Set Medics was born.

For the next few months, as I would continue to build my new business with much success, I would also get the occasional call with an opportunity to "strap on the belt." More often than not, these calls came from Sheri as Kinnie had slowly been removing himself from the business. But whenever I got a call, I would leave work for a couple of days, do a flight somewhere, and then return to my regular routine on the ambulance, which was very much how I had imagined it would be. But one day I received a strange call. Ninety percent of the time when my phone rang it was for work. The other ten percent it was Sheri, offering me a small gig. But this call had nothing to do with either. It was a call from a representative of the Guinness Book of World Records. He told me that they were going to film a world-record flight for a TV show. *Ahhh,* I thought. *They need a set medic.* So I gave him a quote, but he was confused. "I'm not calling you because we need a set medic," he said. "I'm calling you because we'd like you to do a flight. It's for a jet-pack world record." *The Guinness Book of World Records wants me to set one.* But what would be the parameters? Eric already completed a world-record flight for the highest flight, 152 feet, and I had no desire to try to beat *that*. Speed? That was a little dangerous for my taste. So I came up with another option. But I had to talk to Kinnie about it.

I was over the moon. I can't tell you what a shot in the arm it was to share the news with Shelley. I was being given a chance to *set a world record* in something that I had *loved* and would have another accolade to hang on the wall. I called everyone I knew. My mom and dad. My brothers and friends. And, of course, I also called Kinnie, who I was sure would take time out from what he was doing and help me with the flight. Sheri answered the phone and I shared with her the news. And while she was kind and congratulated me on the opportunity, she had some news of her own that tempered my excitement. Kinnie had been diagnosed with lung cancer.

# 17

# Fallen

The Guinness Book flight was scheduled to take place in July 2013. I was upset that Kinnie wouldn't be able to be part of my team, and more upset at the reason why, but I hired my old buddy Dave Kilde and Kinnie's son West to be my team. Shannon, unfortunately, was not available. With the date locked down and the team in place, I couldn't wait to set the record.

Nevertheless, for the few months ahead, two-thirds of my life was in pretty good order. My business, National Set Medics, had started to take off. With my experience in entertainment coupled with the fact that there was practically no competition, I was able to really seize the Dallas market for on-set medics. My part-time gig as a Rocketman looked very promising as well. With a Guinness World Record flight in my grasp, I could cement my place in the pantheon of Rocketbelt pilots. Not only would it assuredly raise my profile, but I was convinced it would also open up other doors that I had wanted to walk through. World records have that effect; I just had to earn it.

During this time, however, the most important aspect of my life, my marriage with Shelley, had begun to sputter. There were several disagreements mounting, but what it boiled down to was that Shelley was tired of what

Rocketman life was doing to me and the moments of pain it had caused. The way she viewed it, my "career" as a Rocketman, aside from being a blast and offering me great travel opportunities, hadn't really done anything for me. Financially, it was a disaster. Yes, I was able to cobble together the money for a small down-payment on a tiny villa. But there were no benefits. No bonuses. No 401(k) plan. No TV show. Nothing. Oh, and there was also the fact that I could've died any time I went up. On top of that, the paramedic job I'd gone to school for only paid $15.83 an hour. She was not happy to learn that paramedics made such low wages. While our household finances were never in jeopardy, we weren't able to save and build a financial future. Shelley felt trapped in a job she would have liked to leave, but because I wasn't earning enough to make that possible, especially now that I was well into my forties, not to mention married and with a child, she just couldn't understand it.

At the same time, I was chapped that *she* couldn't understand *my* perspective. *What was there not to understand?* As crappy as my financial situation was working as a Rocketman, I still viewed it as an investment that would pay off in the future through the speaking engagements I was planning on. And what else was I going to do? I did consider finding a new job even while perhaps still flying the Rocketbelt on the side, but as I mentioned, my résumé was simply not appealing to people in the corporate world. Shelley had no idea what I would or could do, either; she was just worried and perhaps thought she'd hitched her wagon to the wrong horse. But to me, it seemed that she didn't really understand what was my bottom line: I probably would have flown the Rocketbelt for free. It gave me that much joy. And I couldn't give that up. And I certainly wasn't going to quit now while on the cusp of setting a world record. I wasn't looking at it as a choice between flying or Shelley; I believed I could balance both. I made a goal that I would make more money than her. Not out of pride but because that was my job as a man—to take care of his family. I didn't know how this would happen, but I knew if I could achieve this world-record flight, then perhaps other doors would open. So I set my sights on that and gave it all my focus.

---

In setting a world record, as I mentioned, I didn't want to do anything related to elevation or speed. Both of those aspects have very little to do with a jet-pack pilot's refined motor skills. I also felt that if I set the record for either, it would be a very easy bar to surpass. Anyone can fly fast or high. And this fact would also promote what I thought could turn into a very dangerous trend. As the record was sure to accelerate quickly, it would undoubtedly end in disaster for any number of pilots who just wanted to get their names in a record book. With that in mind, we settled on a slalom course that emphasized control and precision over speed and elevation. We then came up with a plan for an open course much like a track, where I would have to fly through it while weaving between three columns and landing at the finish platform. Not to diminish the achievement, but since nobody had even ever attempted a course of that kind on a jet pack, all I needed to do was complete the challenge and I would have a world record hanging on my wall.

The flight was scheduled to take place in California City, California. The producers rented a plot of land, and my flight was one of several acts they were filming that day. Along with West Gibson and Dave Kilde, my brother Steve also attended since he lived only two hours away. On the big day, West and Dave prepared the Rocketbelt for flight while I did a number of interviews. The course itself was far into the desert and at least an hour from any medical care. Being so off the beaten path, I had jokingly told my crew that if crashed into one of the pylons to just send the rescue helicopter because I didn't want to be driven to a hospital.

Although the world-record flight was, arguably, the most technical flight I had ever done, ironically, I don't think I had ever been less stressed about any one flight. Throw out the world record. Throw out the fact that it was going to be televised. For me, the flight was so different than what I had practiced thousands of times. It was something new. With no time constraints, no demanding client, and no unruly crowd to account for, this flight would be a piece of cake. I knew this to be a fact because I had *made* it that way.

---

*"These jetpacks can only remain airborne for about thirty seconds."*

*"So, this guy is, like, in danger of conking out in mid-attempt?"*

*"And crashing."*

This is the kind of exchange the announcers from truTV had to prep its television audience for my flight.

*"Dan has to be totally dialed in to complete the course."*

Well, Dan was "dialed in," no doubt. I *always* was before a flight, and I treated the world-record attempt as no different than any other flight. I prepped. I prayed. And I popped (my clonazepam). Then, after some last-minute interviews with folks from the TV show, I took my position for takeoff and waited for the signal from the Guinness official. The show had a pretty impressive production. There were multiple cameras that covered every part of the course and another camera that was attached to a crane that would follow me around. I even put a couple GoPros on my helmet, chest, and throttle to give the viewers a first-person point of view. Yet as cool as it is to give the viewers a taste of my field of vision while in flight, it can never capture the feeling of being in the corset. Everything on film still looks smaller and slower than it does to the pilot.

*"Rocketman Dan Schlund is about to take off. He has twenty-five seconds to make three turns in a very difficult jet pack, and he's only got thirty seconds of fuel . . . Three, two, one: Go."*

And I went. I lifted off perfectly, elevating to about twenty feet, and started the course. It was a beautiful day with perfect sunshine, and as I began the flight, I was hit with that first rush of dopamine. I was *flying*. And it felt great.

*"There he goes—and that's a nice start!"*

I approached the first tower and flew around it with ease. Next was the more challenging path to the second column where I would have to turn right. As previously noted, right turns had always been a thorn in my side, and it goes without saying that after so many years flying I still had not mastered it. And for this flight, it was no different. Although I was able to veer myself rightward, I left myself with a bad angle for the final column.

*"Oh, he takes that one a little wide!"*

I had. And as a result, I had to "center" myself, turning 270 degrees left again. While this wasn't a big deal, it did eat up several precious seconds of time and fuel. But this wasn't a race, so I took my time, decreasing my speed a bit as I headed toward the last column.

Once I got there, it was another easy left turn to the home stretch. I executed my turn perfectly, then straightened out, spotted my landing platform, and checked my time: twenty-four seconds. Six seconds left. But moving at twenty miles per hour, I had plenty of time to go just sixty feet. Nope, make that fifty feet. *Forty feet.* This was going to be close, but I could now see myself landing. I could see the Guinness World Records certificate framed above my mantle at home.

I began to descend for my landing. I was only thirty feet from the finish—when something happened.

I heard that dreaded sound. That high-pitched hiss of superheated steam I had learned to love suddenly turned into a low-pitched hiss of cool air.

I had run out of propellant, and at twenty-five seconds! I had *never* run out of propellant so early. The timer wasn't even in the red zone. I don't know why it happened. All I can think is that the tanks weren't topped off. We have strict procedures to assure this doesn't happen, and since I wasn't there during the fueling, I can't explain it.

If you want to know what it was like to crash while flying, imagine climbing onto a second-story rooftop, getting on a bike, riding it across the roof as fast as you can, and jumping off . . . with ninety pounds of heavy equipment strapped to your back.

---

When I had my first horrible accident, where nearly a quarter of my body had been seared by scorching jet-pack exhaust, I'd been unconscious for the whole disaster. But now, I did not have that luxury. Also, unlike other smaller spills or poor landings I'd experienced, things didn't happen quickly this time. Instead, I experienced the accident in slow motion. I could, literally, see catastrophe unfolding before me, yet I was powerless to do anything about it. It began with me dropping from the sky at a forward-moving angle and landing on my legs—hard. I'd anticipated this brutal plunge, so I'd prepared myself for impact, slightly bending my knees to absorb some of it. My angular descent was a blessing after all, because had I landed with a straight drop, my legs would have snapped on impact. Instead, when I hit the ground legs forward, they buckled as planned, and I fell forward with the additional momentum, somersaulting up and over as I hyperextended my neck. Fortunately, the Rocketbelt's control arms bore the brunt of the impact to my chest and arms.

On the ground, as the dust settled, I was dazed but still had my faculties about me. It was over now and I had survived. But I knew I'd been badly injured; I just didn't know to what extent. I immediately went into processing mode. Naturally, my first instinct was to get up, but I couldn't. In fact, I couldn't move at all. I felt a tingling in my right hand's pinky, ring, and middle finger, and from paramedic school I knew this meant that I had suffered a neck injury in my C7 vertebrae. In addition to the neck injury, I could see blood on the ground beneath my head. My next memory is of Dave Kilde running up to me. He didn't try to release me but instead yelled, "Medic! Medic!" West and my brother were sprinting across the desert from where I took off.

I wish I could say that the first thing I thought of while I lay on the ground motionless was my family. Or even my health and whether or not I had been paralyzed. But in all honesty, all I could think of in that moment was how embarrassed I was. I had just crashed on an internationally watched television show. And this was TV gold, bound to be replayed on loop and live on in infamy on the internet (which, ironically, it did not). Then I remember my brother appearing next to me. And as all around me crew and medics were working to secure the Rocketbelt and release me from it, I said to them in the calmest voice I could muster, "Take me out. It looks worse than it is." And they did.

As a final, lousy coda to the crash, no, I wasn't airlifted to the nearest hospital via helicopter. I was driven in an ambulance that had bad suspension and no air conditioning.

Advantage: Rocketbelt.

---

The only good thing about my long ambulance ride to Lancaster Regional Hospital was that the paramedic gave me a nice little dose of morphine. I could only imagine how much pain I would be in when it wore off, but by the time we reached the hospital and I was checked in, I was feeling right as rain. One of the nice things about being a paramedic is that I knew what to expect. I knew the tests they would run and the IV catheters I would be poked with. Of course, they did the X-rays and a CT scan too, and it didn't take me long to be told what I had already suspected. I had a small fracture on one of the bones of my C7 vertebrae. Technically, this was a "broken neck." And yes, that sounded awful, but the actual injury was not as bad as it would've seemed; the spinal canal was not compromised, and I would walk again. I called Shelley and told her about the crash and that I was, for the most part, okay. I have a tendency to play down my injuries. Call it being an alpha male. Although I was only in the hospital for a few days, the doctor did not clear me to fly home for a couple of weeks. She was concerned and suggested I quit. I considered it, but I would not make such a rash decision in my current condition. I stayed at my brother's house in Acton, California. And though I was faced with another lengthy and grueling rehab, the only lasting effect would be some minor numbness in the tip of my right index finger. In other words, I had dodged another bullet—at least physically. I could sense, though, that as great as Shelley was in supporting my recovery, her frustration with my enduring commitment to hurling myself through the sky was nearing a boiling point.

And then a new salvo of bullets came from Kinnie. He let me know that he wasn't happy that I made a claim for workers' compensation on the accident. Though it was not an official event through Powerhouse Productions, we had agreed in mediation that I could claim workers' comp if I was injured. I had paid for the use of his Rocketbelt and insurance and two members of his team, including his son, for the flight. I didn't think it would be an issue. But Kinnie thought otherwise. He was old school and believed he held no responsibility for my injuries or any compensation that resulted from them. And though Kinnie would eventually concede, his reluctance to support me and my family after the crash had destroyed any goodwill we had built up after the Angola fiasco. But there was a reason he was aggravated. I later learned that Kinnie, like me, hid a great deal of stress and emotion while he was dealing with his cancer. I didn't know about this and wouldn't find out until a year later. From his point of view, I was just adding more stress to an already stressful situation. I was becoming a liability to his business and his peace of mind.

The final wave of gunfire I took in the wake of my world-record-attempt crash would be the most damaging, and it would also be self-inflicted. Driven by shame, guilt, and self-pity, I would slowly descend into a dark world that made me a stranger to my son and an adversary to my wife. And while I continued on the clonazepam, a new medication would fuel the divide between pain and anxiety: hydrocodone.

# 18

# Saying Goodbye

Time does not heal all wounds. Thinking back on the events of my world-record disaster, failing marriage, business troubles, and drug dependency, I wondered if it would have been better to die. At least I could have gone down in a cloud of smoke and left my family with some money from my life insurance policy. Instead, I was only *half* dead. The clonazepam was not working, and I was completely broke after being released from my paramedic job at CareFlite. My failure had been exposed for the whole world to see. And my failure would be the first thing to pop up for anyone who Googled me. One night, not long after the crash, as all things seemed to be spiraling down on me, I remember a singular moment of clarity. I was sitting by myself in the common room. I don't know what time it was. It could have been in the middle of the night or it could have been in the middle of the day. It was all the same to me. I was high on hydrocodone and feeling grounded. I then remember thinking about Hal Graham, the first Rocketman. This is what he must have meant by "crashed." And for the first time I understood. I understood what he might have felt like as he walked through the doors of his local Federal Aviation Administration office with a .38 tucked into his pants. I understood how he might have felt with his body failing and his career being taking from him and his phone never ringing. And I understood what he might have been feeling after he said hello to the office secretary before pulling the gun from his pants and pressing it to his head. He was a *Rocketman*. He wanted to *fly*. And he *never* could again. Maybe by pulling the trigger he could go to a place where he could—a place that not even a Rocketbelt could take you.

Long after the scabs on my head and elbows had healed, revealing the new skin beneath them, I found myself alone, aloof, and vacillating between bouts of anxiety and fits of rage. But I was neither anguished nor angry at any particular thing in my life. I simply felt beset by a sense of the awfulness all around me. I was injured. I was fighting with my wife. I was fighting with my former business partner, mentor, and close friend, who also just happened to be battling cancer.

At least I wasn't fighting with God. I knew that it was the risk I took and mostly self-inflicted. Many prayers went unanswered; some were simply answered, "Not now. Later." Like my first injury, I knew there was a reason. In my mind I believed that God had to pull me out of this Rocketman persona to rebuild me into someone else. I needed to move on, but my ego wouldn't let me. So, since I couldn't see what the future held, I resisted, and He allowed me to get hurt and took the choice away from me. Years later I'd realize that the truth was, "You're not finished forever. Just for a decade." I felt alone, lost, and abandoned. It didn't help that I also had no money to show for the years of service to the Rocketbelt. I had always known that money did not buy happiness. I was raised by parents who didn't need to preach this, because they lived it. I knew what were the most important things in life. And I knew that money had little to do with any of them. But money certainly has its benefits. And not having it can be a brutal puncture against even the smallest of life's challenges. Had it not been for my son, Danny, I think my life would have been completely devoid of any passion or reason for being.

The biggest problem I faced at the time was all the mounting bills. Between my disability checks and Shelley's new job, we were doing our best to plug the dam, but the holes were everywhere. And there was nothing I could do, because I had not been medically cleared for return to work as a paramedic. After my workmen's comp had initially expired, I would have to apply for an extension every two weeks—which was like a job in itself. And if I wasn't fighting with them, I was fighting with Shelley. Obviously, her working on her own with me splayed out on the couch was not what she had signed up for. And with nowhere to go or nothing to look forward to, the only thing I could do was to take my meds and wait for them to kick in.

I had been prescribed hydrocodone several times after prior surgeries and smaller accidents, and I never viewed it as something that could become problematic. Morphine? Absolutely. Xanax too. But the "hydro," as I called it, was just a meat-and-potato drug for me. It did its job. It took away the pain, and the anxiety too. And in the past, I had no problem stopping it. However, after my Guinness Book crash, it was different—though I don't think it was the crash or the injuries that were different. I think it was because *I* was different. After my previous accidents, I was not only younger and stronger, but I also had a concrete focus, a goal with which I was obsessed, and no other distractions to worry me. Once healed, I would always get back on the horse; but this time, I think both Kinnie and I knew that wasn't going to happen. Before, I didn't have a wife or a child or bills, which allowed me to funnel all of my energy into healing. After my internationally televised crash, I wasn't just broken in the physical sense; the rest of my life had imploded too. You would think that having a wife, a child, and bills would have given me the mental fortitude to will myself out of the hole I had put myself in but, unfortunately, the opposite held true. My failure as Rocketman and my separation from Kinnie made the annoyance of my situation that much worse for Shelley—not to mention her annoyance directly with me. The responsibility I held as father to Danny coupled with my mounting bills only made my anxiety skyrocket. As a result, I began to lean on the hydrocodone not only for my neck pain, but for the calm, however temporary, it brought me. Unfortunately, when the pain from my injury finally receded, it did not take the anxiety with it.

With eventually no pain receptors to soothe, the hydro took over the role of the clonazepam, helping me be patient with my situation, apply common sense with Shelley, and boost my self-esteem, and so I continued on my prescribed dose. The compromise was that, while the drug helped to mitigate my anxiety, soon enough a new emotion began to creep into my life: anger. For much of my life until this point, I'd always been able to keep my anger stored safely on a shelf within me; now, my anger was suddenly bursting into conflagrations while I was under the sway of hydro. And in time, the anger would become a part of me, flowing through my bloodstream like a drug itself. The only emotion that superseded the anger was the anxiety that reemerged when the hydro was out of my system. I was damned if I did and damned if I didn't.

Shelley bore the brunt of my madness. She was the one who walked on eggshells as I either paced about like a zoo animal or rambled on in a drug-induced daze about hating myself. After months and months of living with a man who was clearly no longer her husband, she talked to my mom and Shannon about holding an intervention. In all honesty, I did not know what an intervention was. I had heard of them for sure, and I had supposed that it was some kind of "call to action" to help an addicted loved one. But I always thought it was kind of a low-key, private affair to mitigate any of the embarrassment the addict might feel. As I would soon learn, though, there was nothing private or low-key about it. It's kind of like a surprise party where you go to place and everyone is there to celebrate your life—only it's the opposite. It's like you go to a place and all your friends and family pop out of nowhere and scream, "SURPRISE! YOU'RE FUCKING UP YOUR LIFE!"

I didn't fight it. I had felt in control of the hydro because I was only taking the prescribed amount, but I conveniently ignored the plain fact that I couldn't stop taking it. Shelley and Shannon had set up the meeting at Shannon's house. They knew I needed help and were probably anticipating anger or denial, but I was thankful. Although the intervention made me feel embarrassed and ashamed, I knew Shelley had done the right thing. In my state of mind I didn't know how to move past this. So they did the work for me. Shelley called and invited me over. I didn't know what to expect; I was just happy to see her. After they told me they found a place where I could get off the hydro, I was already ready to get help and thankful they cared enough to find it for me. I could not have done it on my own. So that night, Shannon loaded me and a few of my belongings into his truck and took me to rehab.

---

In June of 2014 I was checked into Eternal Awakenings in Gonzales, Texas, a Christian-based addiction center my family hoped could help ween me off of the hydro. The biggest struggle with that would not be the drug itself but my old friend, Anxiety. Upon admission to the center, I was surprised to learn that I was considered neither an addict nor even a drug abuser. Many of the participants were buying hydrocodone off the streets and some taking upward of fifteen tablets a day—a far cry from my one tablet every four hours. I assumed they thought I was lying. But after close evaluation and tests, the center determined I was simply a person who was taking a medicine as prescribed but couldn't stop. This didn't make sense to me. It was like saying a bank robber wasn't a bank robber, they were just making withdrawals in a manner the bank didn't approve. Philosophy of addiction aside, the center made me go cold turkey (with the help of Suboxone). And though it was a miserable experience for the first week or so—the Suboxone actually left me higher than when I was on the hydro—the center would do exactly what I was checked in for: They would get me off of the drug. I couldn't know at the time that my stay at rehab would end up doing so much more.

The strongest battle I had to fight while at Eternal Awakenings was not with my hunger for my preferred narcotic but with my anxiety. The center was set up to get its patients off of drugs, but it was not equipped to deal with underlying psychological issues. Much of my day was spent either sleeping or trying to relax my mind. At the center, once I finished my withdrawal, I was awash in energy and was up practically twenty-four hours a day. TV was nonexistent. And even after daily sessions, one-on-ones with the therapist, and the varied activities the center offered, I still had a ton of time on my hands. I then made one of the best decisions of my life. To fill out my day—and night—I began to dive into the Bible. Day after day, I swam in the Word. And when I wasn't reading, I was watching sermons online or praying with other people in the facility. I was the closest with God that I'd ever been in my life—and it felt good. This was somewhat of a revelation for me. Though I always had God in my life and I was really good at thanking him during the good times, whenever things got rough, even after my first major crash, I really leaned on *myself*. It's like I didn't want to bother God with my problems. Plus, I thought God had already done enough. I figured He had given me the tools for any kind of mess I created, and all I had to do was use them to figure a way out of my mess. But, I realized that sometimes God needs to remind you that *you need Him*. And when he does, He'll bring you to your knees to be closer to him. And more than ever, I needed to be brought to my knees. I needed God to help lift me out of the state I was in, to give me His wisdom and purpose. I needed to be at His mercy. And so that is what I prayed for, and that's exactly what He did.

While God began to bring me clarity and a new sense of humility, I was still suffering with anxiety and PTSD. With no meds to help combat those symptoms, and with the understandable limitations of the rehab center, I was, in some ways, worse off. There was simply a lot more I needed to do to get healthy again.

Part of that effort involved trying to rekindle my marriage. With my eyes wide open, I was ready to work on the things with Shelley. I had made some big mistakes that had demolished her trust. We really tried hard, but in the end, we were just not able to make it work. So instead, we made a pact: to support one another and continue to raise Danny together in a loving family. Broken as our marriage might have been, we remained united in knowing that Danny's health and happiness was our primary goal from that moment on. And after all, we still loved each other, just not in a married way.

A month and a half later, I returned back to my home, to my wife and child, and I couldn't have felt better. I missed Shelley and Danny so much, and I was determined to make it work with Shelley and right my wrongs. Shelley, for her part, was happy for me but suspect of what might come next. Danny, thank God, was too young to remember this part of my life.

I kicked hydrocodone, but, more importantly, I had experienced the greatest spiritual healing of my life. And to this day, I am still grateful for what the center did for me. In fact, I am now good friends with Jim Welch, Eternal Awakenings' owner, and send the center yearly donations.

---

By 2015, my life had returned to something that resembled normalcy. I went back to National Set Medics and worked hard to rebuild it. And though my days of flying the Rocketbelt were over, I would still get the occasional call from Kinnie to run operations for a show he would book where Eric would fly. At this point, Kinnie's cancer had progressed from his lungs to his brain, and when we spoke, there was always an uneasiness in the conversation. I know there were things he wanted to say, but I'm not sure he could have articulated them given his condition. And I had things to say as well, but I felt that it would have been inappropriate to voice them. In a way, I think that it was best that neither of us found a place to grind our axes, keeping our prior grievances to ourselves. Kinnie and I had been fighting with one another for five years. It was business, but like so many business matters, it was personal too. Kinnie had been a hero to me when we first met. Not only was he one of the great stuntmen and hot-air balloonists of all time, he was also a trailblazer in the field of jet packs. He brought the Rocketbelt out of the subculture of aviation and created the Rocketman persona into the forefront of events and entertainment. Kinnie had, literally, created an industry that still flourishes today. And he plucked me from obscurity to mold me in the Rocketman image. He trained me. Mentored me. He built me into the Rocketman I became. And after my first violent crash, he cared for me too. But Kinnie Gibson had many personas. Aside from his stunt work and his contributions to charities and churches alike—not to mention being the admirable husband and father that he was—Kinnie was also an obstinate, cold-hearted businessman. Unfortunately for me, my business with Kinnie slowly took over our friendship. And while the first half of our twelve years together was filled with joy, camaraderie, and triumphs, our last years were marred with fights, mediation, and resentment.

Sometime in the spring of 2015, I remember bumping into Kinnie at the hangar while I was helping to prep the equipment for a flight in Paris. It had been only a few weeks since I'd last seen him. Despite the cancer, he still looked fit and formidable. We spoke for a moment and caught up, both saying the polite things old acquaintances say to one another when they cross paths. It would be the last time I saw him in person.

On July 19, 2015, Kinnie Gibson passed away. At his funeral was a collection of some of the greatest stuntmen and stunt coordinators in the history of the business. Seeing how much everyone loved him, I was finally able to release the animosity and anger I'd held toward him, and I made sure Sheri and Shannon knew that as well. Kinnie's death seemed to mark the end of an era of Rocketmen. That is why I consider myself "The Last Rocketman." As I thought about this, I began to weep, and I remembered the last thing I said to him.

"See you around, Kinnie."

And I hope to God I will someday.

# 19

# Losses and Gains

After Kinnie died, I didn't fly again. Soon another part of my life would end as well when Shelley and I decided to separate. Much like my own mother and father, there was no doubt that Shelley and I had loved one another deeply, but it was also certain that we could no longer live together. As mentioned, some wounds don't heal. I had finally found a good psychiatrist, Dr. Mohammad Khan in Plano, Texas, who understood my condition and got me on the right medication, but by this time it was not enough. Even though I was finally now ready to step away from it, my years of commitment to being a Rocketman—the bare living I made doing it, the toll it took on my body, and the addiction issues it caused—had slowly opened what was, by now, an impassable rift between Shelley and me. My past mistakes, my addiction and the behaviors it caused, my anxiety, and my still-fledging set medic business remained topics of contention. I couldn't fly anymore, I lost a dead-end job as a low-wage paramedic, and I had no significant savings to rely on. I think it scared her. As her respect for me as a leader seemed to diminish, the closeness between us faded too. By the time I truly got my act together, Shelley had moved on emotionally. Though it was nothing either of us admitted to, it was something I could feel. For a long while, we tried to muscle our way through it. We were both incredibly loving to little Danny and remained civil to one another, but that didn't help to bring life back into our marriage. We discussed divorce, but decided separation would be better for Danny at the time. And if there was one thing we always agreed on, that was what was best for Danny. Shelley would wind up buying a house right down the street from mine, where she still lives to this day. And the three of us remain one of the happiest divorced families you will ever meet.

Despite the relative peacefulness of my separation with Shelley, I was definitely not in a good place. In my life, I had experienced more than a few lows. I had lain in a hospital after nearly being incinerated. I had broken my neck on international television. I had been whisked away to a drug rehab center in the middle of the night by my friends and family because I had been dependent on hydrocodone. And I had to face the PTSD that had plagued me since my first crash. But nothing, and I mean *nothing*, hurt me more than my failure in my marriage with Shelley.

To be very clear, I did not want to end our marriage. But I would be the one who ultimately filed the paperwork. We even went to counseling to learn how to separate well. Though divorce had actually helped my own parents and in all likelihood was one of the most positive things that ever happened in my childhood, I did not want to fail in marriage. I had taken as gospel that given my dogged determination when it came to my goals and endeavors, well, I could actually salvage my marriage with Shelley. And it tore me up.

In my past, depression, anxiety, and self-hatred could always be dealt with. First off, I could stave it off physically. I was in good shape. I could exercise. Lift weights. Sweat. Then, of course, there was the Rocketbelt. There was always the Rocketbelt. And every time I turned that throttle to blast off, I wasn't just releasing an eruption of super-heated steam, I was releasing my own tank of super-heated frustration, self-doubt, and fear, all to be replaced with confidence, faith, courage, and adrenaline. Throw out the exotic travel, the adoring fans, and the raw excitement of being a Rocketman, at the end of the day, it was the rush of flight that filled and refilled my cup. Finally, when I couldn't exercise or wasn't able to fly, there was the hydro. But we all know how that ended. So now, after my marriage had failed, I found myself in what was perhaps an even bigger hole than I had ever been in. And without the ability to exercise, fly the belt, or take the pain medication, how did I deal with it?

Two words: fast food.

While I was never an elite athlete, I was certainly blessed with the physical composition of someone who could excel in vocations that depended on strength, coordination, and agility. At six foot one, I was perfectly sized for stunt work, and at 170 pounds I was sinewy and lithe. And because I had been so incredibly active my entire life, my metabolism was off the charts. I could eat whatever I wanted, whenever I wanted, and however much I wanted, and there was little if any change in my biometrics. But like everything in life, you never see it coming. You think childhood lasts forever until adolescence slaps you in the face. And by the time you even figure out what happened during that, you're an adult, scrambling to find your way in life. As you do that, love shows up and your life changes again. Setbacks, tragedies, and triumphs break up the rhythm of your life until one day you find yourself looking in the rear-view mirror and you realize, all of that is gone. And you're really not even an adult anymore. You're something else. Because you're not a senior citizen. You're something in between. This was a very difficult stage for me—perhaps best defined as a classic midlife crisis. That stage where some men sell their SUVs to go purchase a Corvette. Or some women dye their hair blond and get Botox. Me? I ate fast food. Without the need to stay fit for the Rocketbelt, I was free to eat and do what I wanted.

For starters, let me just state this fact. I'm not a great cook. I don't have the skills and besides, most fast food tastes excellent. And I don't care what's in it. I don't want to know. Secondly, it's not as bad as people think. I'm not going to argue the nutritional value of Subway and Burger King. I'll lose. But many "experts" paint fast food as akin to smoking crystal meth. They even go as far to say it can be an "addiction." And to that I say, I don't know much about many a thing, but I do know I have never seen a homeless person wandering the streets or prostituting themselves because they needed a Whopper. Finally, fast food is cheap. At almost every fast food chain in the country, you can feed yourself for under five dollars. And you can't argue with that.

However, there was a deeper reason I had fallen into my dependence on fast food, besides the fact that it was good, convenient, and affordable. I loved fast food for what it represented. And for me, it represented *youth.* There's no doubt that getting takeout from any place as a child was a major treat. If my mother ever returned home from work holding a bucket of chicken or a bag of cheeseburgers and fries, she was greeted as a conquering heroine by my brothers and me. Every Sunday after Mass, Dad would take my brothers and me to Carl's Jr. When I was editing *Galactic War One* after class in high school, my mom would bring us Del Taco. And as a teenager, there was almost nothing better than going out with my friends, and after a night of driving around, stopping at a Wendy's or Taco Bell or McDonald's, pooling our money and getting as much food as we could. Many of those places even doubled as hangouts as all of us had friends who worked at them, some of whom had the power and sway to "supersize" your order (and what better perk for a hungry teen?). With all of that in mind, every time I ordered fast food, I wasn't just ordering something to fill my stomach. I was ordering memories too. I was ordering my family seated around our dinner table, laughing and smiling as we put our fast food on our dinner plates. I was ordering me and my friends, huddled in a booth over a tray filled with a small mountain of fries with twenty packets of empty ketchup fencing it. And I was ordering the memory of sitting in the drive-through on my motorcycle with the woman who would become my wife as we carefully chose our items because I simply didn't have enough money to get us everything we wanted.

---

Three years and thirty pounds later, the pain from my injury was basically gone, and my anxiety was well-managed with the proper medication. I had survived everything and had no lingering mental or physical scars (save for the weight gain, which I was very self-conscious about, and perhaps some annoyance of having to take the anti-anxiety pills). It had been over five years since my crash, and with Kinnie having passed away, the Rocketbelt was collecting dust at Sheri Gibson's house. While my life had certainly slowed down to a crawl, I was still enjoying it the best I could. And my son Danny was primarily responsible for this. Though Shelley and I had split custody, I was still very much a full-time father. I would help with his homework or we would just go for a walk, and we'd also go on trips. The three of us even continue to have dinners and share holidays together. For all the blessings this life has given me, that boy was the greatest. But it was at this time that something would awaken in me that had been long dormant.

I wrote at the outset that if there was one thing that had been embedded into my DNA and defined my nature, it was struggle. And not just struggle in itself, but *overcoming* that struggle. My grandfather had it. My parents had it. And I had it too. Through everything that had been thrown at us, with help from God, we had overcome it. And we did so with our grit and determination. To that end, failure was never an option. I wasn't a great student with a proclivity toward biology or science, yet I became an exceptional EMT and paramedic. I'm a kid from the valley who had only been on a plane a couple of times before deciding he wanted to be a jet-pack pilot and travel the world. And now, here I was, with my little fledgling company I was running out of my house just to pay the bills, deciding, *I am going to make this work.*

For a long while, National Set Medics could have easily been named Dan the Set Medic. It was just me, booking jobs for myself. But sometime after my divorce and between the fast food, I was seized with the urge to not just grow the business, but really blow it up. I reached out to some of my friends whom I'd worked with when I first got my certification. I figured I could add them to my database and book them jobs too. And so I did. The more jobs I booked, the more productions started reaching out to me for more set medics. In turn, I started recruiting more and more paramedics to my database. Before long, requests weren't just coming in from the Dallas–Fort Worth metroplex, but from out of state too. In fact, it started to get to the point where I couldn't meet demand, so I just kept adding more and more EMTs and paramedics to my database. Growing a company takes lots of hard work and dedication, but I took all the lessons from my previous experiences in the stunt world, as a Rocketman, and in my various other jobs to create an atmosphere of trust and reliability. I was sure to avoid the mistakes Kinnie made with me as well as the mistakes I made with Kinnie. I focused on building trust in my company for my medics and clients alike. National Set Medics gave me a purpose, a direction, and a passion. That coupled with my competitive spirit helped the company to explode. And in a matter of just a couple of years, my database had grown to over 10,000 registered medics located in every state and major city nationwide. And with all of it, finally, something else had taken off in my life: my bank account. And in early 2020, just when I thought business couldn't get any better, it did. The reason was nonetheless something awful for the rest of the world. COVID-19 came.

Unlike most of the rest of the world (besides Amazon and those who sold disposable masks), the COVID-19 pandemic ushered in a windfall for my company. As public health emergency rules and regulations kicked in during the lockdowns, everyone who was trying to flourish and work at this time needed a COVID Compliance Officer (CCO), which was a job that usually fell to the medics. As I already had the database, organization, and personnel in place, we were well-poised to tackle the crisis head on. And for the next two years during the crisis my business grew by 500 percent. In addition to working countless movie sets and construction sites, we also performed thousands of COVID tests on sets and at worksites. We were there to help the industries stay open. It was not just a blessing to me but a blessing to the hundreds of medics we hired and the businesses we helped to keep running. I was shelling out millions of dollars to people who wouldn't have had the opportunity to work otherwise.

By the time all the restrictions and compliance regulations were removed, not only had we become tremendously successful, but the company had made a name for itself that would ensure its long-term success. I was so proud of myself, my directors, and the medics. It was like all the failures and struggles had finally made sense. God did have a plan for me after all, and I was so grateful. Shelley, too, was extremely proud of me. I had achieved my goal of earning more income than her—again, not in spite of her but only to be able to say I was a breadwinner for my son. I was now in a financial position to protect both her and Danny if needed. Shelley was successful and self-sufficient and never asked me for anything from my company during the divorce. But from this success I was able to put Danny in the private school she selected for him. This was something we could not afford earlier. We both achieved our goals. If she needed anything from me, I would be there, and she would be there for me. It is as perfect a divorce as one can hope for if it had to happen. We work together as a team with one goal in mind: Raise Danny to achieve all he can be.

Even before the pandemic ended I was wealthier than I ever imagined I would be. And this was a strange feeling. All my life I'd barely made enough money to get by; now, I could buy whatever I wanted. The good news was that struggling financially for much of my life had made me prudent and smart with money. I wasn't cheap by any means, but I certainly wasn't a spendthrift either. I didn't like fancy things, had no interest in fast cars or anything of that sort. And except for a massage chair, new car, and RV, I invested the rest. The only thing I really spent money on was Danny, because I wanted him to have the best of everything. However, in December of 2020, right in the middle of that windfall for National Set Medics, I did make one more spontaneous purchase that was rather pricey. I was going to my storage unit for some medical supplies and to check on my RV when I bumped into Sheri Gibson. It was the first time I had seen her in years, and it was really nice to just stop and talk for a moment. Naturally, she missed Kinnie, but she and the family were doing the best they could. I shared some of what I had been up to, and we had a nice moment catching up. As it turned out, Sheri was at the storage unit because she had been storing some Rocketbelt gear there and now she wanted to sell one of the Rocketbelts. I asked her how much she was looking for and she gave me the price. I told her I would write her a check that day. Along with the Rocketbelt, I purchased the Rocketman name, the website, and spare parts. Even when Kinnie and I were in the iciest periods of our long relationship, Sheri had liked me and continued to treat me as a friend. I think she felt good about passing Kinnie's Rocketman legacy onto someone who'd been part of the family for so long. I certainly felt honored to do it, and proud that I had raised my income to the point where I could afford to. I believed, as I'd like to think Sheri did too, that I was the only one on earth who could carry forward the Rocketman persona—a clean-cut, all-American, real-life action figure—with the intent and vision Kinnie had established.

Sheri allowed me to choose which Rocketbelt to buy, the red or the blue one. I'd had an ample amount of time with the red one; it was the one I'd trained on, and it was in perfect flying condition. But I had primarily flown the blue one. It's the belt I knew better, and it was gorgeous. But it was still pretty damaged thanks to my crash in the desert, and it looked like it needed lots of work.

I chose the blue one. I didn't care how many times it tried to kill me. It was my favorite and the most beautiful.

Now I had a Rocketbelt but no place to store it. So, I got a storage unit for a few months. But as fate would have it, I discovered that Kinnie's old hangar, where I'd learned to fly and lived for several years, was up for sale. I called for a showing. It was eerie and depressing to enter the place. In a way, it felt haunted to me. And as I looked around, I thought to myself, *No way. Too many bad memories.* But yet there were plenty of good ones too. And there was a poetry to it all. I was returning to my roots. And it just could not have been a coincidence that I had bumped into Sheri and that the old hangar was available at the same time. God was whispering something to me. I debated it internally and talked to my financial advisor. Ultimately, I was reminded that the hangar could also be good for my business as I could store the Rocketbelt, my medical equipment, and even the RV there. Plus, I could rent out the apartments and open hangar space for additional income. So, I made a bid. And after much back-and-forth, I bought it—cash. Mind you, I had no real intention of flying the Rocketbelt again. But now at least I had one. And you don't need to be Pierre de Fermat to figure out what would happen next.

# PART FIVE

# Returning with the Elixir

Who satisfies your years with good things,
so that your youth is renewed like the eagle's.
—Psalm 103:5

# 20

# Nowhere to Land

Nearly a decade removed from my Guinness Book crash, life was good. Very good. My health had returned. My mind was in a good place. My spirit and faith were stronger than ever. And no, I wasn't Elon Musk, but I was rich too. And with the success of National Set Medics, which was just on cruise control, I was getting richer. Little Danny was doing great too. With my additional income, Shelley and I were able to make sure he had everything he needed physically, emotionally, and financially. So, all of that was great, but here's the thing: I was *bored.* I was not built to stay inactive. And I don't really have any other outside interests. I don't follow sports. I'm not a golfer. And though I enjoy an occasional movie, I'm not exactly a cinephile. I needed to do something.

To combat my malaise, I would often schedule myself to supervise on some of the more difficult jobs of National Set Medics. If there was anything with live ammunition, explosives or pyrotechnics, I was there. Or if it was a particular production that involved an adventure, I'd sign up for that too. One such job that I supervised was for the Discovery Channel reality series *Naked and Afraid.* For those not familiar with the long-running series, it chronicles the lives of survivalists who meet for the first time in an undisclosed wilderness location . . . while naked. (I wonder what that pitch meeting was like.) The survivalists are then given the task of staying alive for twenty-one days. I had heard of the show and it sounded like a blast, so I put together a division specifically for high-risk productions such as this called Reality Medics. I then got to wade through the Mississippi Delta swamps (which were much like the Everglades) with the cast and crew. When we weren't in the brush hoping to avoid razorbacks, we were waist-deep in muddy swamp water hoping to avoid alligators. Because of this, we had to be armed with guns too. For a kid from the valley, it was quite the adventure, but I may have been in over my head. At one point, I remember slogging through the hot, swampy landscape when one of my co-medics said, "Come on, Dan. You used to fly with a rocket on your back. This is nothing." I must have looked pretty freaked out. But to this day, I'll gladly take a crash over a gator attack.

In another (safer) way to increase the business of National Set Medics that would still allow me to dial up some much-missed adrenaline, I created a Moto-Rescue division where I and a small group of other paramedics would patrol and monitor marathons on our motorcycles equipped with all our rescue gear. And this ended up being one of my favorite things to do. It was a blast to ride the course with thousands of long-distance runners who ranged in skill from world-class to weekend hobbyist. Running a marathon is an incredible feat for anyone, and it's one of those things that I really wish I could do. But I wasn't given that gift. Had I tried, I would without a doubt been one of the first to need a Moto-Rescue medic. In addition to marathons, we also did bicycle races, and I would lead the one-hundred-mile course three times for the Emmitt Smith Gran Fondo bike race in North Dallas. Lights and sirens blaring.

When my job couldn't supply the adrenaline I needed, at least it provided the money for me to go find it. I took up scuba diving again, and I'd go on to explore the waters of Bali, the Great Barrier Reef, Hawaii, and other incredible locations. I once did Catalina Island, where I had to perform CPR on one of my dive partners. Looking for other kinds of adventure, my brother and I climbed Mount Whitney in California. Mount Whitney is the tallest mountain in the continental United States, and I swore I'd never do that again. Then, with almost nothing left on my bucket list, I decided to take a cruise to

Antarctica, where I would take a polar plunge and kayak below the Antarctic Circle in what was the coldest water in the world. I'd *really* wanted to go to Antarctica, to finally say that, yes, I had stepped foot on every continent in the world. But once I could, aside from my sharing it right now, it's not like it really ever came up in any conversation. And it wasn't as if some lifelong dream of mine had been fulfilled. I was getting my adrenaline fixes in pretty memorable ways, sure, but I found that the thrills didn't last.

It was at this time that I realized I needed to do some real soul-searching. There was no doubt my life had meaning. Fatherhood had given me that. I also had regained purpose and drive. National Set Medics had given me that. But still, something was missing. I should've been happy, right? But I wasn't. It was a corporate job and my background was stunt work and adventure. I didn't know what to do to liven up my life. It was like I was up in the air but with nowhere to land.

In June of 2022 I had a very quiet celebration with my good friend Kevin Baldwin, a fellow paramedic and entrepreneur. I was approaching the date of the ten-year anniversary of my Guinness Book crash. And to mark it, we drove out to the hangar, opened the lock to the Rocketbelt room it was stowed in, and just stared at it. My life had been irrevocably changed as a result of the last flight this belt took. And I had often thought of what my life may have looked like had I had extra fuel in my tank that fateful day. Had I even had those few extra seconds that may have allowed me to traverse that last twenty feet to safely land. And had I managed that, where might have my life then led? While I will never know, prior to the accident I had envisioned myself as a "world-record-holding Rocketbelt pilot." I foresaw fame and speaking engagements and interviews and books. But God had other plans. God saw a father and a successful businessman. And though I would have to go through addiction and the pain of a broken marriage to get there, He got me there. And so, with sincerity in my heart, I say I am grateful for that crash. However, I would be lying if I didn't say that beneath my acceptance and gratitude I didn't also deeply miss being a Rocketman. The Rocketbelt was a part of me, and we would forever be inextricably linked.

To satiate some of my longing for my former life, I toyed with creating a YouTube channel, where I would post some of my old flights and comment on how they came together and what was challenging about them. At the most, I had hoped to garner millions of followers, and at the least, I wanted to share some of my memories. My posts would get a few hundred views and a comment here or there, but nothing that would make me think I was on to something. However, the more I posted and shared, what started to become clear was that I missed being the Rocketman even more than I had realized. I mean, I had thought I was done being a Rocketman—but was I *really*?

It is not hard to convince yourself to do something that you already want to do. First, you assess the hard facts. And in this case, the only true prerequisite for flying a Rocketbelt is having access to a Rocketbelt. Well, I had that. The next thing you need is a place to fly it. Well, I had that too. Then you need propellant for that belt, which, as previously explained, is not something you can pick up at the corner Mobil station. But, I knew how to get hydrogen peroxide. So I bought all I could—220 gallons—and checked that off the list too. The next and final part of the Rocketman equation was also probably the most important: Was I still *capable of flying it?*

Well, I would have to stick a pin in that one for the moment. Because as far as I was concerned, I was ready to fly again. Not just to see if I could do it, but to face the demon one final time and end on a high note. Like Kinnie had always said, "You never want your last flight to be a bad one." I also still had something to prove. Not to myself or my peers, but to my son. I wanted to show Danny what his dad was capable of and that it's okay to fail as long as you get back up. The more I thought of it, the more fired up I got. But there was one other person I needed to show too. And not by coincidence, it was the same person that had made me climb to the top of the Magic Mountain tower: Shelley. Only this time, I wasn't going to do it just to show off. I was going to show I didn't quit on a bad note.

I didn't share my idea with anyone at first. I wanted to get all my ducks in a row before I moved forward. So, I spent a few months purchasing the propellant while also repairing the damage to the Rocketbelt. And while I did, I thought about how I could make the most of my comeback. It was, after all, a momentous event. It needed to be shared. But for that, I knew God would open the right doors when the time was right. And as fate would have it, as I was quietly prepping for my comeback, my friend Kevin Baldwin introduced me to a couple producer friends of his, Angelo Keyes and Eric Dunn. They were looking to make a documentary and searching for a potential subject. Apparently, they had been told that National Set Medics might be the subject they were searching for. So, we all met, and we had a nice conversation, and they were convinced that, yes, National Set Medics might indeed make for compelling content. But then I told them that I thought I could do one better. I then asked them, "How about a documentary about a washed-up jet-pack pilot getting back on the horse after ten years and three near-death crashes?"

# 21

# Lights, Camera, Inaction

When I shared the news that not only would I be making my Rocketman comeback at age fifty-four, but that it would also be filmed for a documentary, it didn't go over quite like I expected. I was hoping for a wave of enthusiasm for my courage and a jolt of exuberance in support from my friends and family. Instead, there was a chorus of vexed apprehension that bordered on dread. This could be summed up by beloved ex-wife Shelley's response, who, after listening to me share my plans, stared at me in disbelief before saying, "Are you sure you're up to this, Dan? You do remember what it did to you and our family?"

It wasn't the response I had envisioned.

Other responses ranged from the indifferent—"Well, if that's what you want, Dan"—to the concerned—"Are you out of your damn mind, Schlund?"—to the curiously encouraging—"Hell, yeah, Dan! Love it! Who cares if it kills you? At least you die happy."

Well, if I died, I certainly wouldn't have been "happy."

The person whose opinion mattered the most was my son, Danny. I doubt there's any father out there who is not constantly worrying about his kid or kids. This is something that is never shared with you before parenthood. From the moment they are conceived, the worry begins. Are they eating enough? Are they sleeping enough? Why are they crying? *What do they need?* And it never ends. Seriously. It. Never. Ends. In fact, for me, it seemed to get worse. I thought I worried about Danny a lot when he was a baby—until he started crawling. Then walking. Then running. Then preschool. Then elementary school. And on and on. So, there I was in our common room with him seated next to me when I pulled him in, *Father Knows Best* style, and said, "Son, there's something I need to ask you about."

Danny had always been a very precocious kid. He was dimensions smarter than I was at his age. Hell, he might have been smarter than me at that time. The boy was constantly reading. He was a whiz at math and could have already worked for the Geek Squad with his knowledge of computers. Naturally, we were complete opposites. Where I was adventurous to the point of stupidity, Danny was cautious. And while I got my adrenaline from activity, Danny received his through knowledge. Danny had known that I had been a Rocketman at one point, but he had no memory of it. He saw the photos and videos but didn't really understand how it had dominated my life. But he *did* understand that it had also hurt me. Although he was only three at the time, he might have remembered me coming home from the hospital wearing my neck brace. And he might have had memories of me convalescing on the couch, nodded out most of the time. And if so, he, in his little mind, hadn't retained many of the darker images that followed: the arguments with Shelley, or my manic fits of rage while on hydrocodone. As a result, I'm sure he did not associate my Rocketman period as days of triumph. Fortunately for me, whatever Danny had thought, they had long been buried in his young psyche. I was just his dad now. I was an overweight, clumsy guy who loved him and took care of him along with his mother down the street. We had a great relationship, and as a father I wanted him to be able to share anything with me. And so when he looked up to me with his most serious twelve-year-old eyes, I said to him, "Danny, I'm thinking of flying the Rocketbelt again. I bought it and have it all fixed up now, and I'm feeling pretty confident. I've got some work to do to get ready, but I wanted to ask you what you thought. I wanted to see if it's okay with you."

This was a half-truth, I admit. I wasn't looking for Danny's permission. But I was hoping for it. His response was perfect in reason and pitch.

"Why?"

Though it shouldn't have, it caught me off guard. I mean, why the hell was I *really* doing it? Like Hal Graham, I had already had an amazing life full of adventure and traveled all over the world. I had done more than I could have ever dreamed of doing. What more could I want? Let's throw in the fact that flying the belt had burnt me, broken me, nearly killed me. It had also indirectly caused my drug dependency, destroyed my marriage, driven me to the brink of bankruptcy. So, yeah, why the hell *did* I want to go back up?

My answer then surprised even me. I had been an administrator for so many years with National Set Medics that I got lazy and comfortable. But there was undeniably a missing component in my life. I was a stuntman at heart. Lying before me was Kinnie's Rocketbelt and hangar, the safety cable, and plenty of propellant. God knows my heart, and He lined me up to continue the Rocketman saga. But how? I knew I couldn't just strap it on and go galivant around the world flying again. I had already lived that life. Maybe it was time for me to train someone else. But how could I do that when I couldn't even conquer my *own* fear of flying?

No stuntman ever wants to end on a bad note, and the failure of my last crash haunted me. I needed to overcome the fear that my second major crash had brought upon me, not only to be able to continue the Rocketman legacy in some way, but also out of sheer ego and stubbornness. I could do this; I *would* do this. I needed to prove to the world, but especially to myself, that I was still capable of being the Rocketman.

Meanwhile, I was still holding onto my vision of carving out a speaking career that would finally make my Rocketman work pay off financially. A documentary and a book would be the investment in myself, my legacy, and my son's future that I had hoped to make so many years ago.

But how was I supposed to explain all that to a twelve-year-old? It was so complicated— and yet, I suddenly realized, so simple.

"I don't want to be afraid anymore."

And that was all it really was. Fear. Fear that I had forgotten how to fly. Fear that I would end my career by failing. Fear that the excitement in my life was over, and that once Danny left I would be all alone like the old lady in the nursing home.

"I know this is important to you," Danny replied. "I believe in you."

Once I closed the deal with the documentary producers, I knew I would have to fly again. That was the Rubicon. Because once they committed to filming and the money was transferred, there was no backing out. Though the story had only been pitched to me, I left it up to the producers, writers, and the director to capture it as is. And I made a commitment to them that I was all in no matter what. I wouldn't hold back on any of the positive or negative aspects of the story or my life. The whole premise of the story was hinging on the fact that I would get back on the belt. If I didn't, there wouldn't *be* a story. The producers loved the idea of the "everyman making a comeback," facing his demon and slaying it. And while they didn't say, "What do we care if you crash trying?", heck, that may have made for an even better story.

But as filming would commence, I had vastly underestimated the emotions I'd be facing, especially regarding personal matters. I had thought that my job would be simple in terms of responsibilities, but I was not even close to being physically ready to fly. To be blunt, I was fat. I didn't just have a "dad bod." I had an "even rocket propulsion cannot lift you" bod. I knew I had to lose weight. And to that end, I had hired a fiery, inspirational trainer to help me do so. Like the Rocketbelt, I had been banged up and collecting dust for over a decade. It's not like I could just throw fuel in my body and fly. I, too had to be fixed, calibrated, and tested until I was in perfect working condition. I figured that I would just do all of that while a camera crew followed me around. But I was wrong. Because the story centered around me, I also had to help organize the entire production. Most of the folks the producers needed to interview were family and friends, so I had to coordinate times and places for those interviews and call in a few favors, even reassure a few people. I had to sift through thousands of hours of footage of old flights and other relevant materials on Kinnie and the history of Rocketbelts to send to the director. Finally, I had to dig up my own history, sharing all the hokey videos I had done with my family, the ambitious but awful films I had done as a youth, as well as incriminating footage of me breaking a number of laws, including my infamous climb to the top of the Magic Mountain tower, and climbing the Hollywood sign. It was exhausting and emotional.

When I wasn't wearing my executive producer's hat, I was being filmed. I had originally thought this wouldn't be a problem. I had been around cameras for much of my adult life, performing or otherwise. But as I quickly discovered, being the subject of a documentary is a whole lot different than being around while cameras are rolling. I had to tone down the Rocketman persona and just be Dan. I liked the director, Jonny Zeller, a lot. He was a smart, artistic Angeleno who had come from the commercial world and had worked with stuntman, motocrosser, and race car driver Travis Pastrana. But I got the impression that he always wanted more from me—to open up to my deepest fears. He probed me like a psychologist and often steered me to places I really didn't want to go. I was embarrassed more times than I could count, mostly with my Rocketman-Plus figure. I also couldn't get used to the camera crew following me around if I went to McDonald's, either. In McKinney, Texas, I'm just another guy, as Kinnie had also been. I was no celebrity. Eventually, I would adapt to the filming and learn to just "rearrange" my schedule for when I knew they would be in town.

While the documentary crew following me around was annoying at times and the production work I had to assist with was frankly a pain in the ass, the biggest challenge I would face while readying for my return to the Rocketbelt was *myself*. As mentioned, I was not just a shadow of my former self. I was something much larger than a shadow. I still looked very much like the old Dan Schlund—only if he were staring at a funhouse mirror that stretched out his gut. And this was something that I was constantly reminded of. Quite literally, almost every person in my sphere of influence who was aware that I was attempting a comeback would all immediately refer to my weight whenever we talked. Even the most mundane conversations began with, "Hey, Dan. How's the weight loss coming?" And it became the de facto central topic of not just the documentary but of my life. It got to the point where it felt like I was on the show *The Biggest Loser*. Everything was about my weight, what I had lost, what I planned to lose, what I was eating. And honestly? It made me want to grab a beer. In fact, before I would make my final and sincere commitment to whipping myself back into shape, I would defiantly go to McDonald's one last time, camera crew in tow.

---

I was incredibly encouraged once my training began in earnest as I viewed it as the single most important milestone of my comeback. You can talk all you want, coordinate schedules, and make promises, but at the end of the day you have to do the hard work. And whipping myself back into shape was going to be key to whether this whole "comeback" thing was going to work. As it stood at the time, I was a good forty pounds over the requisite weight that the Rocketbelt could carry. And as I was informed by a dietitian I had hired, I was at 28.8 percent body fat when, ideally, I should have been closer to fourteen. For the record, I was more than excited for the challenge. There was nobody more bothered by my physical condition than I was. For most of my life, I was so active that it was a struggle to put on weight. There was also a level of vanity that goes with being young that kept me trim and fit. But the underlying truth of my condition at that time was that my priorities had changed a great deal since my Rocketman days. I was now a father first. And as hard as I worked to become a great jet-pack pilot, I did the same to grow my business into what it had become. Honestly, I didn't care about my weight. It wasn't like I was Jabba the Hutt. I had put on a few pounds. But I was committed to taking them off. And I had never, ever taken on something and not achieved it.

My training began at a small gym in Plano, Texas, appropriately called Hidden Gym, and it was the perfect place to embark on my physical journey. A little off the beaten path. No bells and whistles. Just an old-fashioned gym that had everything I needed. I hired a trainer named Kim Lee to help me. She had come strongly recommended by associate producer Angelo Keyes, and she was as advertised. She was a gentle firecracker who didn't mince words and told me exactly what I needed to do and did not like saying it twice. Unfortunately for me, I didn't listen to the first thing she told me.

"Start slow, Dan. We're going to take our time."

Naturally, I thought otherwise. Sure, I was overweight, but I wanted to show her that there was still a dedicated and accomplished athlete deep beneath the layers of fat. So, I went hard and fast. Which was a mistake. It did not take me long to realize I was no longer in my twenties or even my thirties. It also did not help that my knees had suffered from the multiple crashes. I had never remembered working out as being so hard. Or painful. After just ten minutes on the stationary bike, I was gassed and sweating profusely. After twenty I felt nauseous and lightheaded. Still, I remained cool, making small talk with Kim until she finally said, "Time." I then stepped off, nearly buckling, took a swig from my water bottle, and looked forward to some stretching. She then said, "Nice warm up."

Returning home that day, I moved like a zombie in *The Walking Dead*, struggling to climb the three steps of my porch to the front door. I then thought of Rocky Balboa the first time he tried to run up the steps of the Philadelphia Museum of Art. And I wondered, *Am I going to lose this fight?* Staggering into the house, I immediately headed to the bathroom to shower up. And after I took off my clothes, which were sopping with sweat, I once again defied Kim's orders to me when she said with conviction: "Do *not* weigh yourself at home."

Naturally, the first thing I did was step on my scale. I figured I must have lost at least two pounds of water weight. But much to my chagrin, I had weighed the exact same as when the day had started. I was disappointed but not deterred. I had become who I was brick by brick. And I would lose weight the same way. After all, Rocketmen are built brick by brick. And I would not fail.

# 22

# Getting the Band Back Together

We've all seen a movie where some older character suddenly gets the urge to come out of retirement to get back to what he left behind. And to achieve this, he's got to track down his former cohorts and conspirators, all of whom are at other stages of their life and want nothing to do with it. But given our hero's infectious nature, they are persuaded to take "one last ride." Along the way, the audience is treated to these older characters reacclimating to their former lives and squabbling, all the while uttering lines like, "I'm getting too old for this shit." Well, this is kind of exactly what happened as I tried to reassemble my "A team" from my former Rocketman days. This included tracking down my former flight director, Shannon Gibson. Shannon had over forty years' experience as a Rocketbelt technician and was a natural coach. I then convinced my best friend Kevin Baldwin to join. Kevin and I had worked together on many set medic productions and pyrotechnic shows. I knew he could be a great help to Shannon. He was also a perfect person to have at my side. Lastly, I got another technician and stunt coordinator friend, John Cann, on board. John had been partnered with me when Kinnie first chose me to fly. A lot of history there. There were some other great Rocketbelt technicians I loved like

Sid Goodloe and Jeff Ayo, but they lived too far away to help. Anyway, the pitch went something like this:

"Guys, I want to fly the Rocketbelt for a documentary that's being shot. We have to fix the Rocketbelt first, then I have to lose a ton of weight before I can learn how to fly again, and I need your help. Oh, and there's no money in it either."

Needless to say, they didn't exactly jump aboard—mostly out of concern for my own welfare. However, after much persuasion on my part, they were in.

---

The first order of business was that the Rocketbelt needed much more work than I had initially thought. Upon closer examination, the quick-release mechanisms were broken, the support equipment and pumps needed maintenance, and the stopwatch had completely broken off. Most embarrassing, I had to make longer safety straps to fit my increased girth. With the team back together, this technical aspect of my return to flight was in very good hands. However, the mental aspect of my flight was, no pun intended, very much up in the air. Once it became a reality that I was preparing to go back up, the old fear and anxiety also returned. And this was something I was totally unprepared for or thought I had left in the past. I was in such a good place in my life at the time. I had not just pushed all the bad memories of my last flight down to the bottom of my psyche, I had all but forgotten them. But working back at the hangar, "turning wrenches" as Shannon would often say, the anxiety I had left behind returned like a rogue tidal wave. The team picked up on this and did their best to encourage me to help me get my mojo back. And I tried as hard as I could, but it just wasn't happening. It was like I was pretending. I hadn't been physically adventurous in so many years. In short, I got soft and comfortable. I wasn't the hellblazer I once was. To address this, I thought I'd tackle something adventurous, but not as death-defying as the Rocketbelt, in the hopes that it might kindle the flames of my adrenaline. I then decided to return to skydiving because I thought it would help me gauge my anxiety under pressure. Skydiving teaches you to stay calm and trust your ability to control the equipment. Perhaps it's no surprise to say that skydiving was exhilarating. The reason I had left it as a hobby was that after being a

Rocketman, jumping out of a plane with a parachute just seemed tame in comparison. Still, it was a good place to start rebuilding my confidence, so I grabbed my logbook, altimeter, and helmet and ran to the closest skydiving facility in the area: Skydive Spaceland Dallas.

An interesting aside about my skydiving experience is that I never—and I mean never—was afraid before a jump. I may have been nervous, but that feeling was far outweighed by my excitement and training. And I would go skydiving so often and become so seasoned at it that I am ashamed to say that the experience actually became somewhat boring to a degree after a while. I mean, there is a "sameness" to simply falling. Yes, you can learn to maneuver over time, and it's fun to go as a group, but there are not a lot of moving parts to it. You strap into your chute. You get on a cargo plane and fly up. And you jump out. Wash. Rinse. Repeat. Well, I tell you that as I walked into Skydive Spaceland Dallas for the first time in two decades, it was the first time in my adult life that I knew I had *changed.* Obviously, as one goes through life, they undergo many changes. I was aware of that when I had become a married man. And I knew that fatherhood had changed me immeasurably. But even with those changes, I felt that my DNA was very much the same. I was still Dan Schlund. But the moment I walked into Spaceland, and as it occurred to me that I was there to jump out of a plane, I was scared. Still, I covered well, played it cool, and figured the fear would quickly be replaced with excitement after my "second" first jump. I requalified quickly and was ready to go up.

In the past, the instant I jumped, there had always been that feeling of my stomach dropping to my feet, followed by a surge of adrenaline. On this first jump, I did feel a rush, but it was not one of adrenaline—it was indeed fear. But that was okay. I did what I usually did when I tackled something scary: I didn't panic, and I kept on doing it until it felt right. I did about six more jumps, hoping it was just cold feet, but it turned out, it wasn't. Skydiving, apparently, was just something that I no longer enjoyed. While this was revelatory for me, it was also disconcerting. *Will I not enjoy flying the Rocketbelt too?* The answer that occurred to me was yes. But also no. Yes, there was a possibility that my love of flying the Rocketbelt had faded, as love for many things in life dissipates over time. But, no, it didn't matter. I didn't need to enjoy flying the Rocketbelt. I just needed to *do it.*

---

The cable was my second stop on the path to flight—that dreaded, boring, tedious cable. Naturally, I never liked flying on the cable. I don't know any jet-pack pilot who would. It was restrictive, confining, and, in all honesty, I wasn't sure it was the best barometer for flight simulation. Unfortunately, the cable, aka "the tether," was the only way to learn how to handle the Rocketbelt. There was no way around it. Another strange aspect of flying with the cable, besides the fact that I didn't like it, was that I couldn't really recall much about it. There is always some kind of defining characteristic of any endeavor that embeds itself into your muscle memory. But for some reason, this was not the case for flying with the cable. In fact, I couldn't remember much of anything about the cable—besides not liking it. It was either the cable pulled you out of control or you were out of control and the cable grabbed you. It's hard to say which is which. Either way, I probably should have held off getting back on the cable anyway. First, I should have waited until I lost some more weight. Secondly, I should not have allowed the documentary crew to film it. I was opening myself up to potential embarrassment. And I did not disappoint.

I got most of the band together for my first tethered flight. Shannon had made the trip in, and with my other two trusty Rocketbelt technicians by my side, John and Kevin, at least we looked the part. Kind of. It was sort of like seeing one of your favorite bands as a teenager all grown up. As hard as they may try, nobody looks as cool as they once did. I played my part too. I couldn't manage to squeeze into an old Rocketbelt flight suit. So, I just wore jeans and a T-shirt until I could purchase a new one. But the corset—the part of the Rocketbelt that wraps around your hips and back—was not so interchangeable. It was like fitting a banana peel around a watermelon, yet another downside to my extended girth. Once I was finally strapped in and tethered up, I both looked and felt clumsy. In my previous Rocketman life, putting on the belt was like putting on Superman's cape. I really felt like a superhero. Now I felt like a kid on Halloween. Only I wasn't a kid. I was an overweight fifty-something dad. I felt like an idiot, and worse yet, I looked like a pregnant man flying. And to punctuate my humiliation, all of this was being captured on film.

Later, with the crew in their positions and me on my mark, it was the moment of truth. And I then had to do something that I hadn't done in over a decade. I had to turn the throttle. So I did.

I turned the throttle to 100 percent. Most pilots start the throttle low and work up, but I was always a "full throttle" kind of pilot. I had my center, but I wasn't lifting off the ground. *Is there something wrong with the motor? Have I gotten* that *fat?* I gave it a couple of seconds. I have to say, the 160-decibel ear-splitting hiss that screamed from the Rocketbelt was music to my ears. I hadn't heard it in so long and I've yet to hear any kind of audio recapture its overwhelming power. The motor seemed to be running good and hot, so no issues there. Then, finally, after what seemed like too long a moment, I began to lift off and move forward. Although the Rocketbelt seemed to have all the power I had remembered, there was no doubt that my extra weight was a problem for me. And I only managed to go a few feet before the cable grabbed me and threw me out of control. It wasn't exactly an encouraging return, though I'm sure the film crew was thrilled. They had even talked to me before my flight saying, "Dan, it's okay if you can't do it. That's why we want to film it." They called it part of my "character arc." Sadistic Hollywood pricks.

After the camera crew got what they wanted, that is, filming "fat Dan spinning out of control on the cable," they left and the team and I went back to work, doing several more flights at varied levels of success. But on my last flight of the day, as I was lifting off, a cloud of white steam engulfed me. The catalyst motor had blown. This happens when a catalyst is at its end of life. It meant that the Rocketbelt motor could no longer decompose the hydrogen peroxide efficiently and instead shot some peroxide out of the tubes. I immediately shut down the throttle but began to feel a burning sensation in my left boot. My left *leather* boot. The hydrogen peroxide was reacting with the leather. Hydrogen peroxide becomes flammable with any organic material. So, mine caught fire. I started stomping and yelled, "BOOTS! BOOTS!" Kevin was the first by my side with the bucket of water, and John followed with the fire extinguisher. They doused it quickly but not quickly enough to leave me without two huge blisters on my foot. The bottom line was, the Rocketbelt had burnt me again. And the documentary crew was there to film it! Embarrassment number two.

---

When I wasn't being filmed humiliating myself, I was being interviewed for the documentary. And I used the term "interview" loosely. As a professional Rocketman I had done hundreds if not thousands of interviews for a variety of news outlets and content creators. But what I underwent for the documentary was something closer to an "interrogation." The sets were carefully decorated. The lighting was directed on top of me. And the cameras were, quite literally, in my face. As mentioned, the director, Jonny Zeller, was not shy about probing into the deepest recesses of my psyche. I, on the other hand, tried to remain as guarded as possible. It is hard to speak of the more terrifying thoughts only to relive them again before a flight. Yes, I shared what I thought could be shared, but I always held back in sharing my most sensitive feelings—and he seemed to *know* this. The production team went out of their way to loosen me up, even going so far as to film me at my home, in the evening when I was most vulnerable. (They even had beer at the craft services table. Clever bastards.) As much as I tried to resist, at times I know that I probably revealed more than I wanted to. This, in turn, made me very nervous, because if you talk long enough, eventually you might say something you later regret. While I didn't think I said anything disparaging about anybody, as time went by and the cameras kept rolling, I couldn't be entirely certain. Midway through filming, when my entire focus should have been on losing weight and continuing to hone my skill on the belt, I was worried that perhaps, in the heat of the moment, I might have said something that might hurt someone's feelings. *Maybe I sound too bitter about Kinnie . . . Maybe I didn't give Shelley enough credit . . . Maybe I shouldn't have shared anything about my parents . . .* I also had interviews where I had been drinking. How would *that* come off? All of this was just noise, but it was noise that I didn't need at the time. All said, I did promise to be completely transparent, good or bad.

I was most at ease when the camera crews were not around. So, whenever they returned to Los Angeles to film other segments of the documentary, I was able to breathe a sigh of relief. But that wouldn't solve my problems altogether. I still needed to lose weight—and I wasn't. Oh, I was still working out like mad, and Kim continued to drive me hard, but all the stress of the documentary had made me want to eat (and drink) more. And though I had been on a strict diet, I sometimes snuck in junk food and trips to McDonald's. After about a month into my routine, I had lost only a few pounds. However, I was getting stronger, and my aerobic condition was increasing. I was even able to point to the fact that my body fat had actually decreased. Though this was encouraging, the only thing that matters when you're trying to lose weight is that you *lose weight*. And everyone needed to see more results.

If there is one thing that film production and flying a Rocketbelt have in common, it's that time is money. The more time spent in preproduction, filming, and postproduction, the more expensive the film becomes. I understood this. The more time we put into our shows at the Rocketman organization coordinating, practicing, burning fuel and the likes, the less money we simply made. We didn't get paid by the hour. Same goes for a film production. They begin with a certain budget, make the schedule, and then do everything they can to abide by that schedule. Obviously, documentaries are a little trickier because they are more fluid. Still, they abide by the same principle of staying within the budget and staying on schedule. And as filming for my documentary eased into the fall of 2023, several warning bells would go off. First off, I was still not even close to going back up. Because the Rocketbelt needed constant maintenance, I wasn't able to manage a consistent workload of practice, and fuel was limited. Just like I had been trained back in the day, I had to relearn in increments, which dramatically slowed down my pace. But even had the Rocketbelt been perfect, I still was far from ready because, again, I was too heavy. The ideal weight was less than 180 pounds, and I was sitting at 215. After a month with Kim the trainer, I'd dropped to 200, but with the holidays around the corner, I was eating a little more than normal and drinking beer to calm my nerves. It was a race between my commitment and my growing anxiety. As every week passed, I could feel the collective tension of the producers who wanted their film "in the can." And I could feel the pounds collecting.

Naturally, the producers' anxiety eventually found its way to me. After all, I was the subject of their documentary. By now, they had done all of their interviews, had sifted through all of my previous flights, and had a pretty good grip on what the story was. But after nearly four months of shooting, what they didn't have was an *ending*. It was going to end in one of four ways. I was going to do the Guinness Book flight and get it right this time, or I was going to do *any* successful free flight—or I was going to crash, or I was going to chicken out. The filmmakers needed to prep for all scenarios. So nearly every week, if not every other day, someone from the production team would reach out and say with all the enthusiasm of a car salesman, "Hey, Dan! How are you feeling today?" Translation: "Hey, Dan. When the hell are you going up?" And I always told them the same thing, answering politely: "I'm doing good. And I'm almost there. I just need to finish [A, B or C]." I didn't know what else to say. I was doing my best. Nobody wanted me to go up more than me. Still, I felt badly for them. I felt that they had bet on their horse and I had let them down. I was *going* to go up. I just didn't want to make them any promises with a hard date. Still, I got it. They wanted action. They wanted to film something that might stir the pot a little bit and I needed some help. Something or somebody with a little color and energy. I gave it a thought and then gave them exactly what they wanted. I called one more member of the old band.

Eric Scott is the best Rocketbelt pilot there ever was. He moved in the air like a hawk, spinning in flight, diving and turning on a dime, and always leaving a filled stadium stunned in awe. As mentioned, he also holds a world record for the highest human flight with a Rocketbelt at 152 feet—something I wasn't interested in even considering.

It was the perfect opportunity to bring him in. First off, I knew Eric would offer me great moral support. He had always been a friend first, and if anyone could understand what I was going through, it would be him. Secondly, I didn't want the documentary to be just about me flying, and I thought Eric would bring a much-needed energy into the production. And true to form, when he showed up at the hangar, I felt good. Eric, who like the rest of us looked a bit older and moved a pinch slower, still had that ease and confidence and swagger about him that we had always loved him for. He was just cool. And the moment he showed up with his big, toothy smile wearing a T-shirt with cut sleeves (naturally), it gave all of us a much-needed boost. He had also matured a great deal since those wild days when we were younger. Pulling me aside, he offered heartfelt words of encouragement and wisdom.

Then he gave me some encouragement of a different kind. He offered to give the Rocketbelt a try with its new catalyst pack and no tether. And with the cameras rolling, Eric strapped up as if he were trying on a pair of shoes, hit the throttle, and flew right up. While he may have been rusty by his standards, it was an impressive flight for someone who just walked off the street. After landing, as everyone on the team, myself included, slapped his back and the documentary crew guffawed at his ability, Eric nonchalantly announced, "Well, it has plenty of power!" Then he joked, "No dents in the machine, or myself!" Naturally, I wanted to go bury my head in the grass. He made it look so easy.

Then, for good measure, I did something that was long past due and meant as a special gift. I let Shannon Gibson strap into the Rocketbelt and give it a spin on the cable. In all his forty years, he was never given the opportunity to "turn the throttle." In all his unique insights and training, he never got to experience the thrill himself. Kinnie's excuse for barring him from the experience was always, "I'd never close the casket on my brother." But I thought the cable was safe enough. And damn if he didn't deserve it. He did great too. He didn't get the height he wanted, but he experienced the thrill of flying the Rocketbelt nonetheless. His most poignant comment was: "It's heavier than I imagined."

Now it was my turn to do a flight. I was hoping to do my free flight with Eric there.

As they were fueling up the Rocketbelt, Kevin noticed that one of the safety restraints was loose. We attempted to fix the problem but determined that it was not something that could be fixed without re-milling the piece. So, again, I had to tell the producers that I couldn't fly. Another delay, another costly repair. Yet in a small way I was relieved. Nonetheless, I went home later that day feeling worse about myself. Obviously, the real long-term problem with the Rocketbelt was me. Even at 180 pounds in my prime, I was on the heavy side—not for my height, but for the belt. Eric weighed a trim 150. Now, even after weeks of training, I weighed in at a pudgy 210 pounds. And the holidays were upon us.

# 23

# And Then There Were Three–Endings

I can't ever recall being as excited about a new year as I was for 2024. Now that I had made that decision and there was a film crew documenting everything, it gave my life a spike of adrenaline that I had long lost. That was the good news. The bad news: After the holidays I was actually heavier than I was before I began my training.

My lack of progress in shedding pounds became a huge scare for the production team. After all, it's hard to make a documentary about a guy who wants to fly a Rocketbelt one last time but can't because he's too fat. How does *that* story end? To be honest, I thought the filmmakers wouldn't have minded if I crashed, as hard as they were pushing me. And I suppose that would've been an exciting ending, but it certainly wasn't the punctuation to my story that I wanted. The good thing for me was that another problem had sprouted up that was also stalling production, one that quite frankly I was happy about as it took the attention off of my weight. Producers were having a difficult time getting a date and securing the proper releases for the world-record flight. Obviously, times had changed over the years, and getting the proper permits along with dealing with organizations and insurance and all sorts of other moving parts really made events like a Rocketbelt flight very difficult. So, while the film team haggled with that, I snuck away and finally did what I needed to do. I got back in shape.

Back in the day, when I and the team were at the top of our game, sponsors used to throw money at us. And as one who would rarely say no to extra money, Kinnie took as much in as he could. As a result, I would often fly with a sign or a placard hanging off my body. Or my helmet would be custom painted with a logo from any one of many high-end brands. Heck, there were times I looked like a NASCAR driver with all of the brand patches slathered over my flight suit. But if there were a sponsor for the world-record flight I was prepping for, it wouldn't have been Visa or Coca-Cola. It would have been the Red Mountain Weight Loss program. It was with their help and some of the meds they prescribed that I was able to shed my "fat suit." Oh, it took some work. And I pretty much went to a liquid-based diet (not Bud Light this time) for a whole month. But between that and my never-say-die trainer, I lost sixteen pounds in just over a month. I looked and felt great. It wasn't quite the forty pounds I'd originally intended to shed, and I had not quite met my goal of 200 pounds, but I was light enough for the belt to lift me.

---

There's something incomparable about a free flight. No matter how much you practice on the cable or how many hops you do to perfection, it can never match the sheer thrill of being off-tether. The thrill is contagious, as well. It's something the whole team can feel—they're a part of it too. It is because of their hard work and commitment that any pilot achieves liftoff and flight. And on the morning of my first free flight in ten years, this shared feeling of accomplishment was palpable.

Before my flight, Kevin and I had to repack the catalyst motor. This was the last catalyst pack we had, which meant the belt only had about fifteen to eighteen flights left before we had to replace it again. Obviously, this was a very difficult and expensive prospect that took three different manufacturers to produce, so whatever we needed to do to get me back up, we needed to do it sooner rather than later. There would be no extensive training period as there had been before I became a pilot. This added yet another ticking clock to the whole endeavor, however much it actually pleased the production team.

Now it was time to lock down the details of the flight. I had discussed with the producers from the onset of the project that the documentary could only end in one of four ways. One: I would get back up in the air and do the Guinness Book flight, thus conquering my demon and putting a bow on my Rocketman career. Two: I would successfully complete a flight, but it would not set a record. Three: I would attempt the flight only to spectacularly crash, capping off my career in tragedy. Or four: I'd simply chicken out. The fourth option wasn't impossible to conceive. I went through each scenario, thinking deeply about exactly what it would look like.

Maybe I get back up but can't do the world-record course because my skills have diminished . . .

Maybe I crash, but it's not a bad one . . .

Maybe I just injure my knees or ankles . . .

Or maybe I finish and crash at the end—a Pyrrhic victory.

I realized that there was one thing I didn't need to consider, which was backing out. There was no way that was going to happen. It didn't have anything to do with the documentary or my ego or the danger involved. The truth was the same thing I had shared with little Danny when he asked me why I was going up again. I had to go up *for me.* I knew then that this was *the whole point.* It wasn't for a record or a documentary or to add another notch to my Rocketbelt. I was going up because I *needed* to go up. I needed to prove to myself I could do it. And even if no one had been in my corner, and even if there was no film crew documenting it, I was *not* going to end on a bad note. I was going to go *up*! And I didn't care if I had to do it in the middle of the night and there was nobody around to see it. *I was going back up.* As I realized this, it felt like one of those "cue inspiring music" moments. It was an epiphany.

Beneath this core drive remained a foundation of various motivations. As a father, I wanted more than anything to do this for Danny, to show him who I'd been. And even beyond my son, there was something else that nobody could see, something that truly gave me the confidence that I was going to achieve what I had set out for. And that was God. I had lived long enough to realize that God is involved in our successes. And as I grew as a Christian and began to reflect on my life in an honest way, I came to realize that, by design, God's fingerprints were all over my failures as well. This doesn't mean that He caused them but rather that He *allowed* them to happen so as to bring me closer to Him. Every hiccup I had ever had in life always brought me to a better place, a place where I was closer to God and more at peace with myself. And ironically, there was a direct correlation between the difficulty of my struggles and the spiritual growth that resulted from them. Every valley I fell into—no matter how deep—always brought me to a greater summit. Among other things, my flight would be a way to acknowledge all I had gained through my relationship with God.

The first few free flights for all Rocketmen are always the most dicey. And it is no coincidence that they are also the flights when most pilots crash. Having fallen and been incinerated on just my third flight, this was obviously something that I knew firsthand. But as I prepped to fly my first "off the cable" flight in a decade, I didn't have any of the confidence or swagger I possessed during my training as a youth. This was a *good thing*. There's an old saying in aviation, "Ignorance is the best teacher." In other words, if you truly don't understand how dangerous something is, you won't approach it with any trepidation, which leads to error. But in this respect pilots come in all shapes and sizes. Some, like Kinnie, were able to build a healthy fear and respect for the Rocketbelt that allowed them to succeed, while others, like Eric, seemed to be missing that "fear gene" altogether. I had to constantly fight with the fear. And what I had learned in my experience as Rocketman was that I could never conquer fear; however, I could *manage* it, mitigate it by staying in control and not allowing myself to panic. I knew what the Rocketbelt was capable of. But I also knew what *I* was capable of. When I was dialed in I was as good as any pilot there ever was. But flying the belt was like a chess game in my mind, and I needed to stay at least three moves ahead. The bottom line is that in my older age I had replaced swagger with mental fortitude. But truth be told, I would have given anything for some of that old bravado.

My profound drive continued to wrestle with my apprehension, but my mind remained fixed on the accomplishment. I was ready to present the talents that my master, God, had given me, and my prayer was that after I had achieved my goal, I would hear, "Well done, Dan."

But before I had this chance to realize my prayer, I was given stunning news. Producers had called. Because of a number of obstacles and permits that they could not overcome, they were unable to secure and schedule the flight. The world-record course was off.

*Now* what was I going to do?

To be honest, all of me felt relief, though I didn't share that with anyone. I had been pushing myself too hard too fast and for too long. I knew it was God's way of saying, "You're not ready." I needed more practice, more weight loss, and more money for extra catalysts. I also knew what I really needed to do: just fly the belt one more time, and then decide what my future would be. In short, don't skip steps. Baby steps from one accomplishment to another.

It would be the easiest decision I ever made. I was a Rocketman. I was simply going to fly.

And I was going to enjoy it.

# 24

# Staring into the Abyss

With the world-record course off of the table, we met with the film production crew to discuss alternative flight plans. And with each passing suggestion it became crystal clear to me that the filmmakers now saw the flight as less about a "man conquering his demons" and more about production value and spectacle. Well, after a career of doing just that, I shot down every idea that came my way. My ego said yes, but my mature self knew to say no. Which wasn't easy. The flight, I told them, was about nothing but that—the flight. That's what it was *always* about. To that end, I made a very simple decision. I needed to go back to the beginning, back to where it almost ended before it even started: the hangar where I had done my first free flight and was nearly burnt to death after crashing. I wanted to look into the abyss. Would it be a spectacular scene? I supposed not. Would there be undeniable production value? Frankly, I didn't care. I just wanted to fly and land on the very spot that almost ended my life and career. And to be quite honest, I was struggling to do even a test hop. I needed to start small and build myself back up. Piloting the Rocketbelt (to say nothing of achieving a spectacular flight in the process) after so much time requires almost a beginner's training. When we were initially planning the documentary, I thought my comeback flight would be easy—strap the belt on and pick up where I left off.

That was not the case.

---

Over the years spanning my career, I experienced a number of what'd I'd call "the most important flights of my life." Obviously, the first one off the cable in Miami was a biggie; it christened me as a Rocketman. And, of course, the flight at the Rose Parade in front of my family and four hundred million people was huge too. Then there was the one for the *Star Wars* convention when I got to dressed up as Boba Fett, a personal dream. Then our wild experience in the former Soviet Union. And on and on. And as I reflect back on my days of flight, it seemed almost every other week was "the most important flight of my life." But on the night before my return to the Rocketbelt for my first free flight in over a decade, it occurred to me that this flight truly was *the* most important flight of my life. And this terrified me as much, if not more than, my first free flight in 2002.

And so there I was the night before, and there was my anxiety, back to say hello yet again, unbothered by all the progress I'd made in the past. To probably no surprise, I was upset that this old scourge had returned at this moment. It wasn't like I was *afraid* to go back up. Of course, I wondered to myself if would I be sleeping in my own bed the next night or a hospital bed, but that's not what kept me up. The truth was simply that I was afraid to *fail.*

Though I never knew this, there is actually a word for "the extreme fear of failure": *atychiphobia*. Had I been aware of this widely shared phobia in my younger years, it may have helped me cope with my own anxiety with the Rocketbelt—especially because at the end of the day, it wasn't about the Rocketbelt at all. Almost my entire life had been spent performing for others. I put on shows for my family. I made films for my schoolmates. I became a stuntman to bring joy to audiences. Hell, I illegally climbed a tower to impress a girl. All of my anxiety stemmed from the fear that if I failed, I wouldn't be *liked*, that I wouldn't be worthy.

But deep down I also knew that I was still in many ways that eighth grade kid who understood his purpose: to entertain. The only person I could fail was myself—and I knew that wasn't something I needed to worry about. Having figured all this out after hours of staring at the ceiling, I slept the rest of the night like a baby.

I met the team at ten a.m. at the hangar, and everybody was already there and working. Shannon and the crew were prepping the Rocketbelt and going over the flight path. The documentary crew had already shown up too and was prepping the cameras. I, on the other hand, had nothing much to do after showing up and happily greeting everyone. And though I was offering to help with this and that, I was always given the same response: "You go relax, Dan. Focus on the flight." And so I would go to my RV, my de facto dressing room, and wait, say my prayers, and in the process of waiting, slowly lose my mind—but this time, not with anxiety or frustration. As I reacquainted myself with this preflight routine, for the first time in my career I didn't feel like an insolent child with ADD waiting to go out and play. It was the opposite. I was overwhelmed with excitement and fear, both at the same time. It was like I was reliving the most exciting periods of my life. As we all know, it is always the best of times that go too quickly. From the innocent freedoms of childhood to courting the girl of your dreams to watching your child grow up, many of life's joys are already mere memories before you can even savor them. But sitting there by myself in my makeshift waiting room brought back some of my fondest memories, one of those being hearing the din of my crew working without me.

The time came and I started getting dressed, taking in the smell of my flight suit and the exciting anticipation of going up. The only thing that was missing was the noise of a crowd outside, that amazing buzz and hum from an arena or stadium or rows of stands. I was now a crowd of one. This flight was for me and me alone.

Rocketbelt flights are timed to the minute, and in most cases, to the second. And per protocol, we had always employed a meticulously planned schedule. This is what inspired the business name T-Minus Productions.

At t-minus 60 minutes before the flight, we'd fuel the Rocketbelt.

At t-minus 30 minutes I would get into costume or the flight suit.

At t-minus 15 minutes I'd set the pressure and heat the motor.

At t-minus 10 minutes I would strap in.

At t-minus 5 minutes I would disconnect from the stand and proceed to my takeoff position.

That last part was always the most important. It's tough to stand waiting more than five minutes with over 160 pounds of rocket motor and propellant on your back. This too was something I had conveniently forgotten, just how damn heavy and uncomfortable the Rocketbelt was. And as I stood waiting with it on my back, I swear to you, it seemed much heavier than I had remembered. But now came the hardest part: the sheer moments before takeoff.

It takes a long time to master the mental part of a preflight routine. When I was a young Rocketman, all I could think of was hitting that throttle. That was, literally, the only thing on my mind. But as I grew into a professional pilot, I took those last moments and used them to really *envision* the flight before it took place. I pictured myself from the moment of takeoff, lifting off, accelerating. In my head, I had to own everything around me, land and air. I also reminded myself that I was absolutely independent. My team had done their job, but they were done now, except for my Reality Medics division, who I flew in just in case. It was now my turn to do my part. All of my practice and preparation, and the documentary itself, hinged on this moment.

Obviously, this wasn't like my flight in Brazil that spanned three hundred yards in front of a hundred thousand people. I was just doing a short hop from the tarmac to the location where I'd almost been burned to death. The planned flight was to do twenty yards and then, if all went well, do a turn and make it another fifty yards. I wouldn't know until I got in the air.

I got the notice from Shannon that we were ready. It was now time for my second "first free flight."

Before the countdown, we had to wait for a cue from the production team. Director Jonny Zeller, whom I'd now grown very fond of, had planned a really cool drone shot that would sweep over the course. I could hear its faint buzz approaching when I got the signal from Shannon. And I did what I had been waiting to do for over a decade: I turned the throttle, not for a tethered training round, not for a short test hop, but for a real flight with a small audience of friends in attendance—this included all of the personnel from my first crash.

In the past, I would always lift off just after hitting the throttle, the thrust reliably immediate and powerful. But for a good moment I didn't budge after I hit it. I was just still too heavy. But here's where it gets tricky: At the moment of thrust, you have to hold your balance perfectly as you wait to lift, a challenge not unlike balancing on a beach ball while holding two fire hoses. It almost happens in slow motion. It took a few seconds for me to lighten as we burned off fuel weight and a few more seconds before my feet finally left the ground. I elevated up to about fifteen feet and then began moving forward . . .

It was controlled and perfect—so much so that I immediately was struck with another urge: to *gun* it. And I was just about to when my own voice popped into my head: "No ego, Dan. Just fly." And so I did, staying the course and keeping to the simple A-B-C plan. Lift. Go. Land. Just like my first free flight in 2001. And so that's exactly what I did. I might have come in a little hot, but I nailed the landing to a smattering of applause from my crew and spectators. I couldn't have been happier.

That was until Jonny approached with bad news. "Hey, Dan," he said. "Nice job, but we didn't get it. The drone was out of place. You took off too soon." So, I'd simply misread the "go" cue and set off prematurely.

I was demoralized because it was a great flight, and if anyone was watching closely, they may have caught it. But then Jonny said, "I know you want to go back up anyway, Dan." And then yelled, "Back to one!" And he walked away.

I stood there like an idiot for a second, until it struck me. He was right. I did want to go back up! So back to one we went.

Twenty minutes later, we had refueled the belt and I'd added more pressure to the tanks to help with liftoff. I maxed it out, and then maybe a bit more. Everybody took their places and there I was again, standing, waiting, ready to hit the throttle, emboldened with confidence by the success of the previous flight. I decided that the "missed shot" was probably a blessing. I was going to make this flight even better. All this effort to miss the shot? The production needed it and damned if I didn't want to do it again.

We awaited Jonny's signal. The signal came—the *actual* signal this time—and I hit the throttle. Again, there was no immediate liftoff, but this time I became engulfed in a cloud of white steam, a sign that the catalyst was now spent—but I wasn't ready to call it quits; we needed the footage. It was now or never. It would work for this one last flight—whether we got the shot or not—but after that it would need to be replaced (and as it turned out, the extra pressure I'd added had fouled up that catalyst for good). I held the throttle full blast and, after a moment, I slowly lifted out of the white cloud like a phoenix. I then did exactly what I was supposed to do. There was no urge toward speed or elevation; I just wanted to focus on control—and it was perfect. Not Boba Fett perfect but Dan Schlund perfect.

As I approached my landing spot, I came in hot and in a pinch, and in a case of petrifying déjà vu the moment I hit the ground, I started to bounce, having not shut off the valve quickly enough. This was exactly what had caused my crash-and-burn decades earlier. But as soon as I felt my legs start to lift off the ground again, I quickly shut it off and came to a gentle rest. There was no way I was going to relive that nightmare of bouncing and crashing.

Again, there was a smattering of applause from my crew. And all attention turned to Jonny, who was reviewing the drone footage on one of his monitors. After a few moments, he calmly removed his headset and approached, taking his place in front of us. We all then waited for the verdict when his face bent into a smile.

"We got it," he said. "Congratulations."

Success! I immediately called Danny and Shelley to let them know I was okay and that it went well. They came by after school to hug and congratulate me. Our family celebrated. I had made my son proud.

Later I took the entire Rocketman team and film crew to Buffalo Wild Wings to continue the celebration. Beer was back on the menu.

# 25

# Never Landing

No dream lasts forever. I think that sometimes knowing when to let a dream go, whether you've been living it or have never reached it, is the hardest part of life. Ask any actor or artist who is still waiting tables in their forties. Or that aging athlete who has lost a step but is still holding onto his or her career. I was no different. I pushed the envelope and was lucky to have survived to talk about it. Age is, in the end, undefeated. But if there is a silver lining to getting older it is being able to look back on your life and have clarity. I truly have very few regrets. One realizes that life moves in seasons: childhood, adolescence, adulthood and career, and family. And while "adventure" is a great part of all of these seasons, many people treat it as if it is a season unto itself, one that must wait until old age or be abandoned after youth. They wait until retirement to travel the world. They wait until they are old to buy the car of their dreams. Sometimes they even wait to love the people who are closest to them because they're too busy during their other seasons. While I am far from perfect, I do take solace in the fact that at least I didn't wait. Adventure was a part of every season of my life. I had traveled most of the world before I was forty. I stepped foot on every continent. I was one of less than a dozen people to have ever professionally flown a Rocketbelt. And I have loved my God, my family, and my friends with unlimited zeal. Yes, I have fallen. Repeatedly. Spiritually, psychologically, legally, and, of course, physically. But I was always able to get up, and I always had help when I needed it. What a blessing. In fact, as I look back, sometimes I really think I never "fell" at all, that the challenges and failures were just part of a long, necessary, inevitable process—and that since taking off, I'd never really landed. But the thing that I really learned was that, just like the seasons of our lives, "adventure" continually changes too.

After the 2013 crash, I thought I had to give up adventure and with it, my identity. After all, my body was banged up and heavy. My spirit was weak. My marriage was struggling, and I had a son to look after. So, I unstrapped the Rocketbelt and buckled up to a desk and a computer monitor. I thought that I was giving up a dream but really, I wasn't. For a long time I kept comparing my old life to my new one and there was just no way paying invoices while owning National Set Medics was going to compare to strapping on a Rocketbelt and flying in front of hundreds of thousands of people. But the more I thought about it, there was also nothing that could compare to picking my son up from school and seeing his smiling face as he slid into the passenger seat of my car. And though my marriage with Shelley would ultimately dissolve, she remains one of my closest friends. She had been with me through it all—and still is. From Magic Mountain to Rocketman and beyond. And as unspectacular as it may seem, there is nothing that could compare to the feeling I have providing livelihoods to hundreds of men and women all over the country who have made a career out of being set medics and are grateful for the work. Through this I realized that God helps to ensure we never really "lose" our dreams. Instead, He replaces them. God had to tragically pull me out of the Rocketman persona because He had better plans for me. But the great thing about God is that He didn't say I was finished. When the time came and the time was right, he rewarded me. He gave me that opportunity to fly the Rocketbelt one last time. Buying Kinnie's old hangar and his Rocketbelt was something that He knew would come to pass all along, but we don't get the luxury of knowing His plans ahead of time. That's why it's called faith.

Even today, I still want to fly. The roaring belt and the open skies still call me. I'm drawn to that incomparable rush like the tide to the moon. And I know that I'll get calls in the future to strap on the belt and fly again. But I now know my limits. I pushed the envelope and survived. And as much as I'd like to say yes to those calls, alas, I will choose each time to pass. That dream no longer exists for me. It has been replaced with others, including writing this book. While the documentary shares some of my story, I wanted to address the parts of my life that the documentary couldn't show. I am hoping that sharing my story might provide some inspiration for any person who has dreamed and still wishes for adventure in their life. And I am hoping that I can translate my experiences as a Rocketman, as well as the stories I've told here and in the documentary, into a career where I can continue to inspire others not just as any anonymous Rocketman, but as Dan Schlund, *the* Rocketman.

There has been talk about passing the torch and training another Rocketman or . . . Rocketwoman? And there was a brief moment where I had hoped that my son, Danny, might want to carry on that legacy. But if I were honest, I'd let him fly on the cable only. As Kinnie once said about his brother Shannon, I refuse to close the casket on anyone because of *my* dream. One of the most amazing things about fatherhood is watching your child grow into their own dreams and adventures. Danny is not a risk-taker like I was. He's more of a thinker. He's the kind of person who builds Rocketbelts but doesn't fly them. And as I continue to watch him grow, I am overwhelmed with joy and gratitude for how God has worked through my life.

As a boy, I always looked to the sky and dreamed of adventure. As a young, ambitious, adrenaline-junkie adult, I made a living in that sky, flying all over the world. But now as an older man and a father, I look to the sky and I just see God and his many blessings.

Maybe that's why I wanted to spend so much time up there.

# Index

# About the Author

**Dan Schlund**, known worldwide as "The Rocketman," is a seasoned stunt performer and one of the few individuals in history to master the Rocketbelt—a rocket-powered device capable of human flight. With a background in stunt work, he has worked as a paramedic, a licensed pyrotechnician, and a producer of live stunt show entertainment, carving a unique path that took him from California theme parks to international stages and screen appearances. In his time as Rocketman, Dan booked and performed countless Rocketbelt flights in over thirty-five countries across six continents, including producing the world's first water jet-pack performance for the 2012 World's Fair in South Korea.

The Rocketman may be Dan's most notable persona, but it is only one small aspect of his many unique skills. Dan's businesses include both global and national clientele. In the 2010s, Dan started his business National Set Medics, a collection of over 11,000 like-minded EMTs, paramedics, and other emergency medical service professionals who provide producers of TV, film, and events affordable, turnkey emergency medical service nationwide.